589 264 0295

1000

Retail Graphics

ROCKPORT

GLOUCESTER MASSACHUSETTS

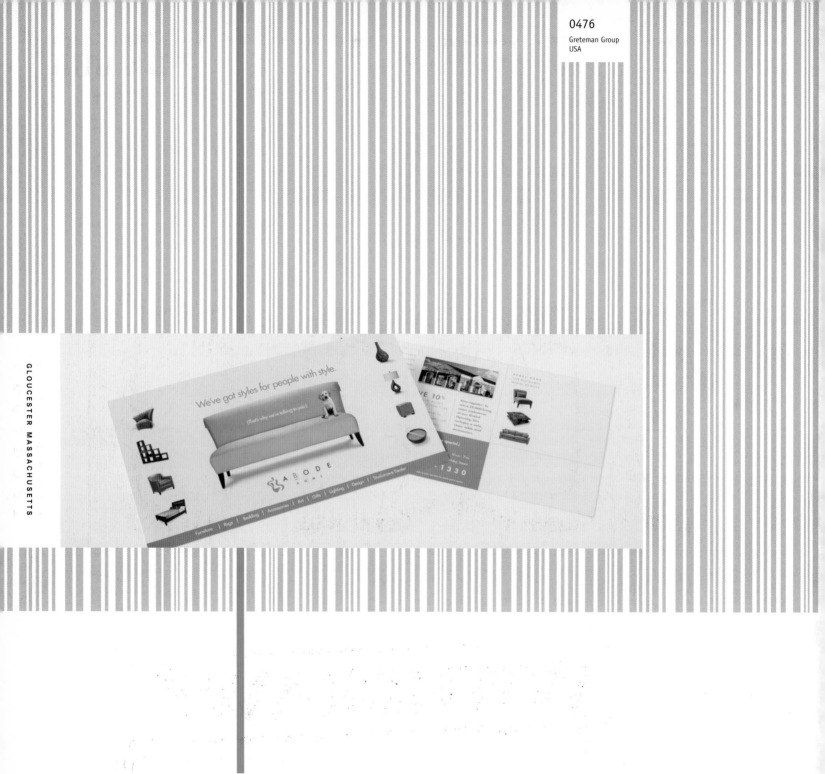

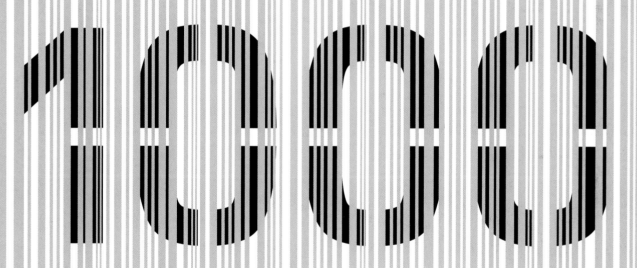

Retail Graphics

ROCKPORT PUBLISHERS

From Signage to Logos and Everything In-Store

ISBN-13: 978-1-59253-336-7
ISBN-10: 1-59253-336-1
349346
10 9 8 7 6 5 4 3 2 1

First Published in the United States of America by
Rockport Publishers, a member of
Quayside Publishing Group
33 Commercial Street
Gloucester, Massachusetts 01930-5089
Telephone: (978) 282-9590
Fax: (978) 283-2742
www.rockpub.com

JGA Chairman   Ken Nisch, JGA
Project Director   Marcy Goldstein, JGA
Book Coordinator   Holly Barrette, JGA
Book Design   Brian Eastman, Beastman Creative
Cover Design   Brian Eastman, Beastman Creative

Printed in China

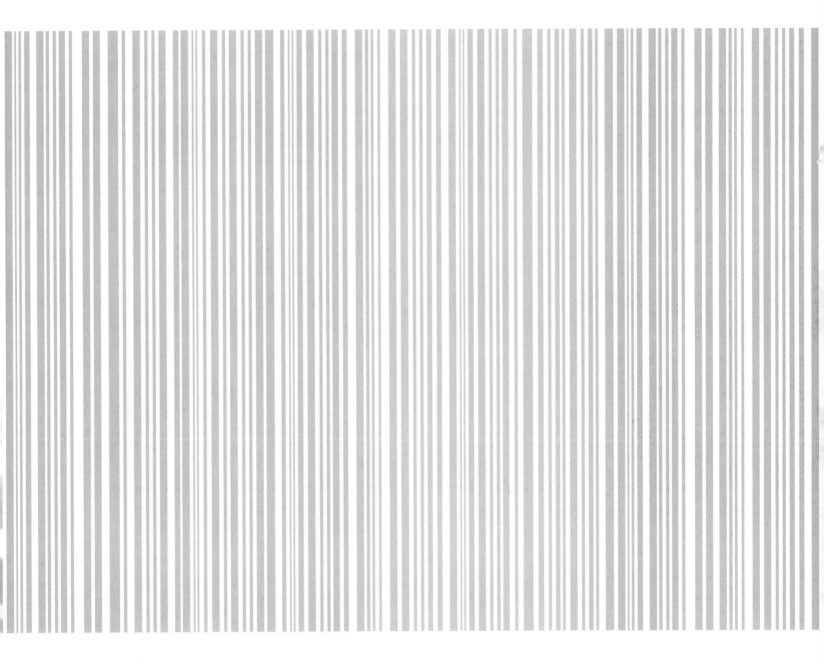

741.6 SUT

CONTENTS

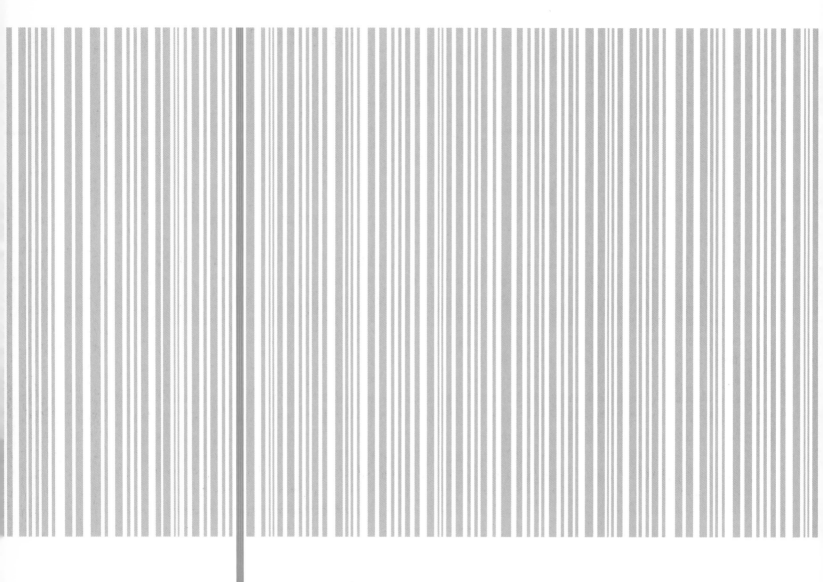

 JGA.

THE BUSINESS OF DESIGN   THE ART OF PARTNERSHIP

INTRODUCTION

The bar code, seemingly ubiquitous, is also individualistic. Think of it as the fingerprint of the commercial world—a language that in its short history supersedes most spoken languages in the way of communicating, not only between machines and computers, but also amongst people, commercial entities, and products themselves. Bar codes are used to "speak" and connect with consumer behaviors, gathering their buying habits and processing that information to create a dialogue that communicates electronically with shoppers.

Like bar codes, graphics are part of a global language that transcends the words that separate cultures. Images of a smiling baby, a cuddly puppy, and even the human body in its most exposed and unadorned ways, can say many things to many people.

In looking at these 1,000 examples, we note how the diversity of the bar code—the fingerprint and the image—can connect, provoke, befuddle, and clarify the communication from one entity to the other. If, in the words of designer Ambra Medda, "designers are the new rock stars," then graphics are the lyrics, and the essence of the music with which these design rock stars communicate.

Each surface of every visual is in its own right a form of communication, whether intentional or not. These 1,000 touchpoints of brand identity—promotional and printed materials, packaging, signage, and environments—while highly intentional, act as the headlines, punctuation, and in some cases the subtext of the surroundings in which they exist. Much like the bar code, they surround us, structure our access and understanding, and bring additional meaning to the world in which we live.

—Ken Nisch, Chairman, JGA

0033
Mindseye Creative
India

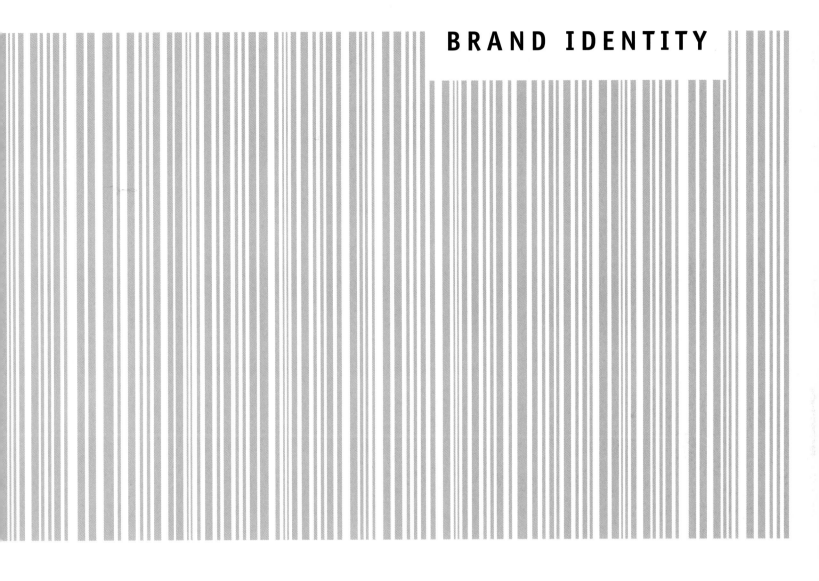

BRAND IDENTITY

-0120

Communication Arts
USA

MAASMECHELEN VILLAGE

OUTLET SHOPPING

0002 Communication Arts
USA

0003 Communication Arts
USA

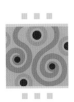

INGOLSTADT
·VILLAGE·

OUTLET SHOPPING

0004 Communication Arts
USA

Wertheim Village

OUTLET SHOPPING

0005 Communication Arts
USA

0006   3
USA

0007   Lauriedesign
Switzerland

Museum of Science

0008   Minelli, Inc.
USA

Tallulah Belle's

0009   Jake Burk
USA

bennett schneider

specialty greetings & paper

| 0012 | Entermotion Design Studio
USA |

| 0013 | Entermotion Design Studio
USA |

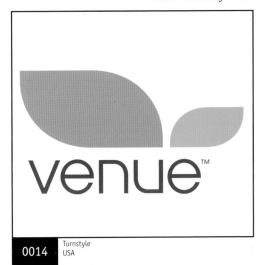

| 0014 | Turnstyle
USA |

| 0015 | Hollis Brand Communications
USA |

| 0016 | Hollis Brand Communications
USA |

| 0017 | Hollis Brand Communications
USA |

| 0018 | Casella Creative
USA |

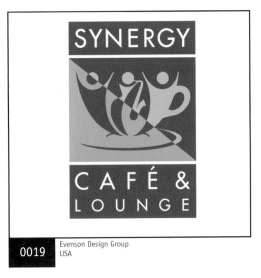

| 0019 | Evenson Design Group
USA |

| 0020 | Evenson Design Group
USA |

0021　Vrontikis Design Office
USA

0022　Vrontikis Design Office
USA

0023　Sayles Graphic Design
USA

0024　Sayles Graphic Design
USA

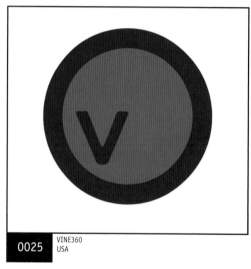

0025　VINE360
USA

0026　Riordon Design
Canada

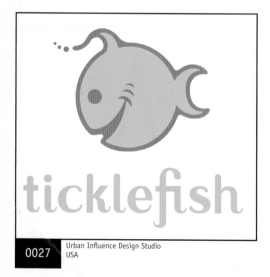

0027　Urban Influence Design Studio
USA

0028　I. Paris Design
USA

0029　Landini Associates
Australia

Evenson Design Group
USA

| 0032 | Landini Associates
Australia |

| 0033 | Mindseye Creative
India |

| 0034 | Landor Associates
USA |

Red Ambrosia
FINE SENSUAL GOODS

| 0035 | Arcadia Studio
USA |

the natural way to a healthier future

OPTIMUM HEALTH
NEW ZEALAND LTD

Julia Davidson, Medical Herbalist - NZAMH
Optimum Health Clinic, Severne St, Blenheim
Ph / Fax: +64 3 578 7335
Email: clinic@optimumhealthnz.co.nz
www.optimumhealthnz.co.nz

0036   Lloyds Graphic Design
New Zealand

0037   Cubellis Marco Retail
USA

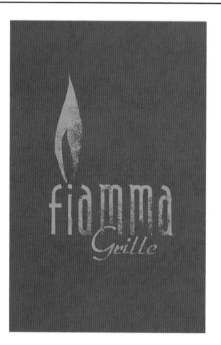

0038   Cubellis Marco Retail
USA

0039   Hardy Design
Brazil

0042   Hardy Design
Brazil

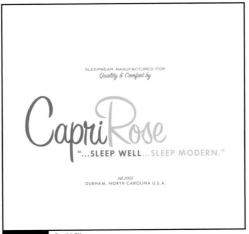

0043   David Eller
USA

0044   Hardy Design
Brazil

0045   Greenmelon, Inc.
Canada

0046   Greenmelon, Inc.
Canada

0047   Hardy Design
Brazil

0048   ALR Design
USA

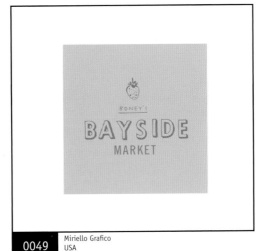

0049   Miriello Grafico
USA

0050   Jeff Fisher LogoMotives
USA

0051 Desgrippes Gobé
USA

0052 Desgrippes Gobé
USA

0053 Wallace Church, Inc.
USA

0054 Michael Calleia
USA

0055 Michael Calleia
USA

0056 Hollis Brand Communications
USA

0057 Greenmelon, Inc.
Canada

0058 R&MAG Graphic Design
Italy

0059 R&MAG Graphic Design
Italy

Nocturnal Graphic Design Studio
USA

A B O D E

H O M E

| 0062 | Greteman Group
USA |

PLATERIA RAFAEL

SILVER FACTORY SINCE 1970

| 0063 | TD2, S.C.
Mexico |

Joshua Tree
GARDENS

| 0064 | Whitney Edwards, LLC
USA |

| 0065 | Matcha Design
USA |

redsnail

| 0066 | Kinesis
USA |

THE OUTLETS AT
VERO BEACH℠
FASHION, STYLE & MORE

| 0067 | Kiku Obata & Co.
USA |

COVENTRY
MALL

| 0068 | Kiku Obata & Co.
USA |

McKINLEY
MALL

| 0069 | Kiku Obata & Co.
USA |

ZEHNDER'S
MARKETPLACE

Z · JAVA CAFE

ZEHNDER'S
MARKETPLACE

Z · CHEF'S CAFE

ZEHNDER'S
MARKETPLACE

Z · BAKERY

ZEHNDER'S
MARKETPLACE

Z · BAKERY

ZEHNDER'S
MARKETPLACE

Z · BAKERY

ZEHNDER'S
MARKETPLACE

Z · GIFTS

ZEHNDER'S
MARKETPLACE

0072   Up Design Bureau
USA

0073   HG Design
USA

0074   Brand Engine
USA

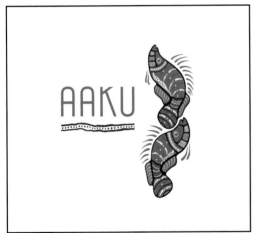

0075   Brand Engine
USA

0076   Brand Engine
USA

0077   Brand Engine
USA

0078   Brand Engine
USA

0079   Grafik Marketing Communications
USA

0080   Grafik Marketing Communications
USA

0081   Sayles Graphic Design
USA

0082   Sayles Graphic Design
USA

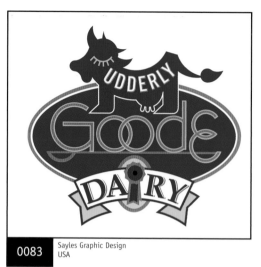

0083   Sayles Graphic Design
USA

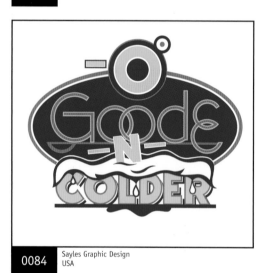

0084   Sayles Graphic Design
USA

0085   Sayles Graphic Design
USA

0086   Sayles Graphic Design
USA

0087   Sayles Graphic Design
USA

0088   Sayles Graphic Design
USA

0089   Sayles Graphic Design
USA

IKEA
Sweden

0092   Bamboo
USA

YOUR ELECTRICAL SUPPLY SOURCE

0093   Wave 3
USA

0094   Krispy Kreme Doughnuts, Inc.
USA

0095   Greenmelon, Inc.
Canada

blue tulip

0096   JGA
        USA

TORRID

0097   JGA
        USA

ARTE & FRANK

0098   Frost Design
        Australia

METROPARK

0099   JGA
        USA

BRIGITE

BRIGITE

BRIGITE

BRIGITE

BRIGITE

Charney Design
USA

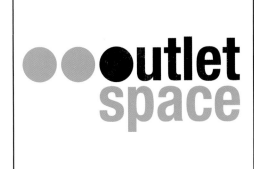

0102   3rd Edge Communications
       USA

0103   Landini Associates
       Australia

0104   Landini Associates
       Australia

0105   TrueFaces Creation Sdn Bhd
       West Malaysia

0106   28 Limited Brand
       Germany

0107   ARTiculation Group
       Canada

MedBiz MARKET

outlet space

0108   CFX Creative
       Canada

0109   Hollis Brand Communications
       USA

0110   R&MAG Graphic Design
       Italy

0111   Gardner Design
USA

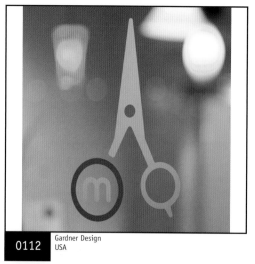

0112   Gardner Design
USA

0113   Life is good.
USA

0114   TrueFaces Creation Sdn Bhd
West Malaysia

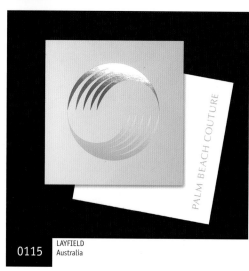

0115   LAYFIELD
Australia

0116   Gabriel Kalach - Visual Communication
USA

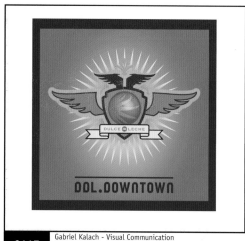

0117   Gabriel Kalach - Visual Communication
USA

0118   Gabriel Kalach - Visual Communication
USA

0119   cincodemayo
Mexico

Muggie Ramadani Design Studio
Denmark

From Left To Right
Andrew – Franz Stripe Shirt: Grape $79.95, Pseudo Jacquard Jumper: Black $89.95
Richard – Jacob Stripe Shirt: Black $79.95
Michael – Image Dobby Shirt: White $79.95, Lithium Vest: Black $59.95
Martyn – Hayden Stripe Shirt: Espresso $79.95, Pseudo Jacquard Jumper: Blue $89.95

TAROCASH
www.tarocash.com.au

0127

Landini Associates
Australia

0121

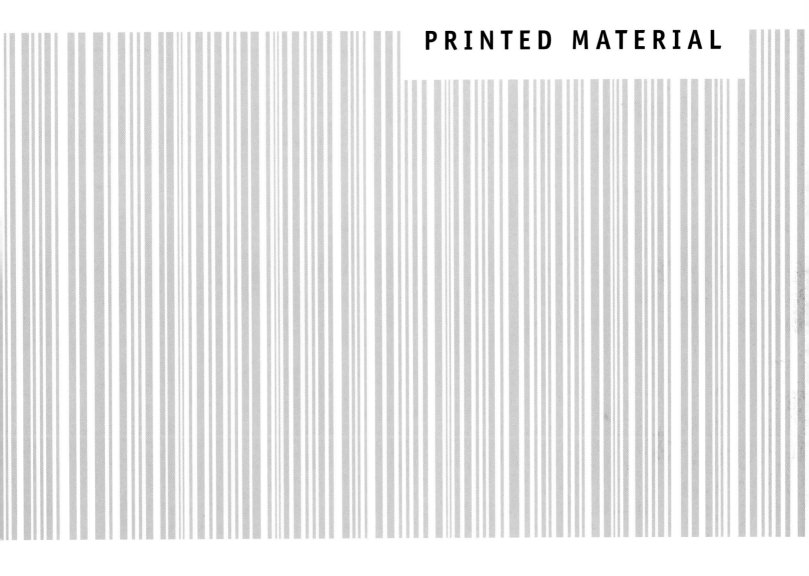

PRINTED MATERIAL

Design Ranch
USA

0122 Design Ranch
USA

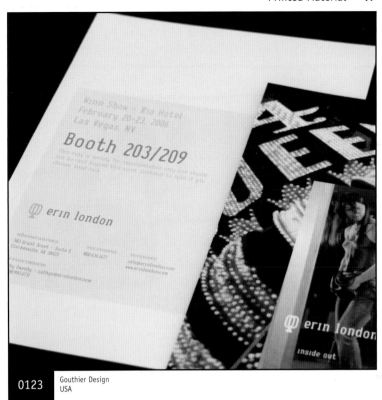

0123 Gouthier Design
USA

0124 Gouthier Design
USA

0125 Landini Associates
Australia

0126   Landini Associates
Australia

0127   Landini Associates
Australia

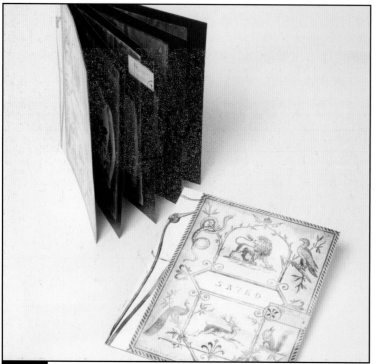

0128   Nothing: Something: NY
USA

0129   Nothing: Something: NY
USA

0130 Nothing: Something: NY
USA

THOMSON ™

Crisp Retailing Smarts™ Series

Decaf

Shots

> NRF
FOUNDATION

Explaining Features and Benefits

Selling and Promoting Products | WORKBOOK 5

U.S. $11.95 CAN $15.95

ISBN 1-4239-5071-2

Thomson Course Technology
USA

0132 Thomson Course Technology
USA

0133 Thomson Course Technology
USA

0134 Thomson Course Technology
USA

0135 Thomson Course Technology
USA

0136 Thomson Course Technology
USA

0137 Thomson Course Technology
USA

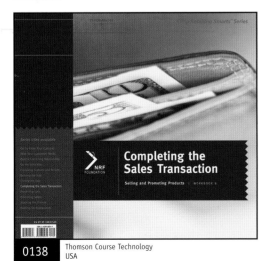

0138 Thomson Course Technology
USA

0139 Thomson Course Technology
USA

0140 Anders Malmströmer Grafisk Design
Sweden

0141 Geyrhalter Design
USA

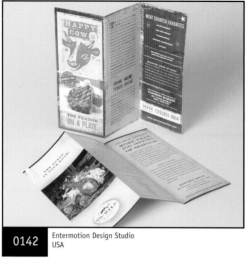

0142 Entermotion Design Studio
USA

0143 Design Ranch
USA

0144 Design Ranch
USA

0145 Design Ranch
USA

0146 Design Ranch
USA

0147 Gardner Design
USA

0148 Gardner Design
USA

0149 Templin Brink Design
USA

Nothing: Something: NY
USA

Nothing: Something: NY
USA

0153 Nothing: Something: NY
USA

0154 Nothing: Something: NY
USA

0155 Hardy Design
Brazil

0156   Hardy Design
       Brazil

0157   Hardy Design
       Brazil

ESSENCIALE INVERNO 2005

0158   Hardy Design
       Brazil

0159   Hardy Design
       Brazil

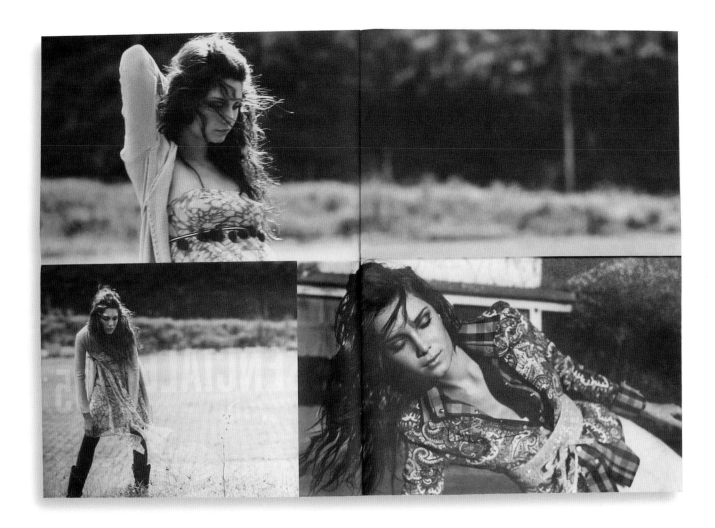

bloodorange

0162   Hardy Design
Brazil

0163   Hardy Design
Brazil

0164   Hardy Design
Brazil

0165   Hardy Design
Brazil

0166   Muggie Ramadani Design Studio
Denmark

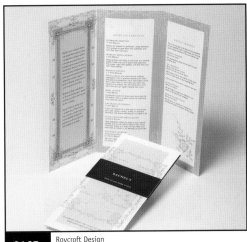

0167   Roycroft Design
USA

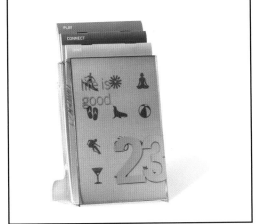

0168   Hollis Brand Communications
USA

0169   Hollis Brand Communications
USA

0170   R&MAG Graphic Design
Italy

0171 TrueFaces Creation Sdn Bhd
West Malaysia

0172 Revoluzion Advertising and Design
Germany

0173 Revoluzion Advertising and Design
Germany

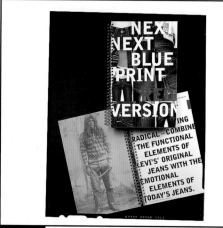

0174 Morla Design
USA

0175 Templin Brink Design
USA

0176 Templin Brink Design
USA

0177 Gardner Design
USA

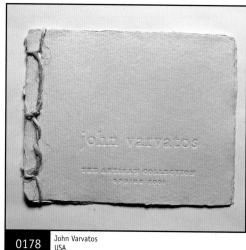

0178 John Varvatos
USA

0179 John Varvatos
USA

New Pioneer Co-op
june sales

chill

Honeydew Melon
White Tea
$12.99

Select Herb Teas
$1.99

Select Organic
Sorbets
$2.69

Select Organic
Bottled Teas
89¢

june 1st–14th
$9.99/lb.

MAVERICK RANCH
All-Natural
Boneless Ribeye

New Pi SEAFOOD
$5.99/lb.
Fresh Atlantic Salmon
Fillets

hello, summer
june 15th–30th
$1.99/lb.

New Pi MEAT
All-Natural Pork
Country-Style Ribs

New Pi SEAFOOD
$7.99/lb.
Swordfish Steaks

0182   Fitch Worldwide (London)
        UK

0183   New Pioneer Food Co-op
        USA

0184   New Pioneer Food Co-op
        USA

0185   Ellen Bruss Design
        USA

0186 Gardner Design
USA

0187 Gardner Design
USA

0188 Gardner Design
USA

0189 Gardner Design
USA

0190   Design Ranch
        USA

Design Ranch
USA

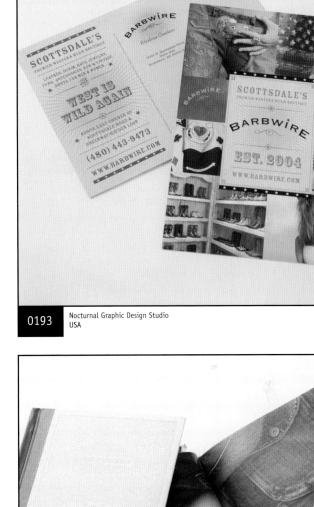

0192 Ellen Bruss Design
USA

0193 Nocturnal Graphic Design Studio
USA

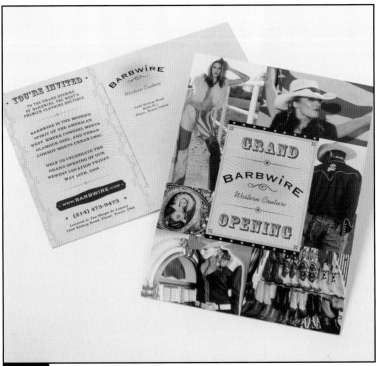

0194 Nocturnal Graphic Design Studio
USA

0195 Design Ranch
USA

0196 Gouthier Design
USA

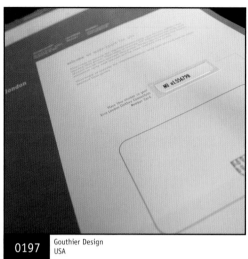

0197 Gouthier Design
USA

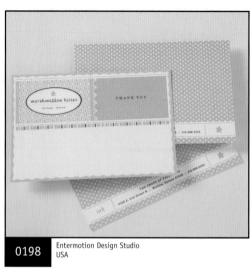

0198 Entermotion Design Studio
USA

0199 Riordon Design
Canada

0200 Nocturnal Graphic Design Studio
USA

0201 Nocturnal Graphic Design Studio
USA

0202 Hardy Design
Brazil

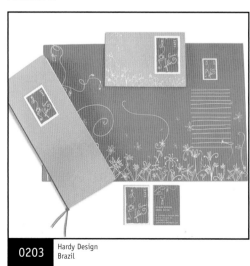

0203 Hardy Design
Brazil

0204 Nothing: Something: NY
USA

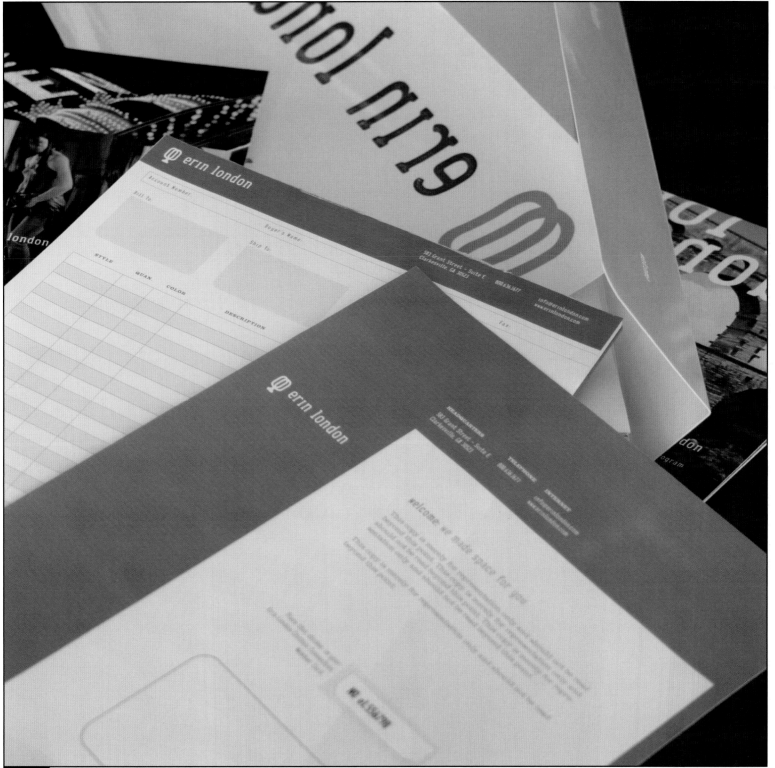

Gouthier Design
USA

| 0207 | Hardy Design
Brazil |

| 0208 | Hardy Design
Brazil |

| 0209 | Taxi Studio LTD.
UK |

| 0210 | Muggie Ramadani Design Studio
Denmark |

| 0211 | Gardner Design
USA |

| 0212 | Gardner Design
USA |

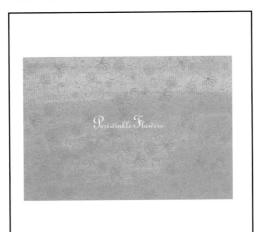

| 0213 | Gardner Design
USA |

| 0214 | Pylon Design, Inc.
Canada |

| 0215 | Design Ranch
USA |

0216   Graphic Content
USA

0217   Graphic Content
USA

0218   Hollis Brand Communications
USA

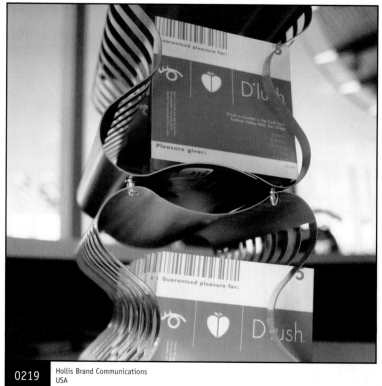

0219   Hollis Brand Communications
USA

Design Ranch
USA

Ellen Bruss Design
USA

Riordon Design
Canada

0223 Landini Associates
Australia

0224 Nocturnal Graphic Design Studio
USA

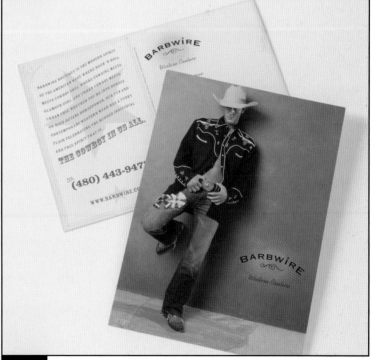

0225 Nocturnal Graphic Design Studio
USA

Nocturnal Graphic Design Studio
USA

0227 Nocturnal Graphic Design Studio
USA

0228 Nocturnal Graphic Design Studio
USA

0229 Nocturnal Graphic Design Studio
USA

0230 Nocturnal Graphic Design Studio
USA

0231 Nocturnal Graphic Design Studio
USA

0232 Nocturnal Graphic Design Studio
USA

0233 Nocturnal Graphic Design Studio
USA

0234 Nocturnal Graphic Design Studio
USA

ART + CLOTH + ORIGINAL THOUGHT

and

ELLAS · ITALIA
FABRE

p.Dejulio

DUAL-DEBUTS @ THE RENEGADE: SEPT. 24 + 25 / 11A - 6P
150 indie designers in the middle of Wicker Park (1425 N. Damen)
FIND OUT MORE @ RenegadeCraft.com

Good Night TV
USA

Haus der Bücher
BUCHKAISER
Karlsruhe   Kaiserstraße 199   (0721)   92 92 9-0
Karlsruhe   Waldstraße 47   (0721)   92 92 9-0
Landau   Gerberstraße 23   (06341) 91 77 1-0
Landau   Marktstraße 89   (06341) 98 75 5-0
Rastatt   Poststraße 12   (07222)   3 23 48
www.buchkaiser.de

0237	thinkDESIGNco USA

0238	Templin Brink Design USA

0239	Landini Associates Australia

0240	Landini Associates Australia

0241 delphine
USA

0242 Trainor Design
USA

0243 Hartford Design
USA

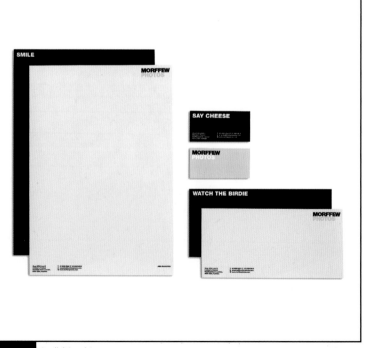

0244 Landini Associates
Australia

Wolken Communica
USA

Entermotion Design Studio
USA

0247 Design Center
USA

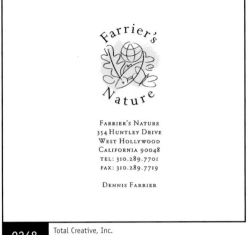

0248 Total Creative, Inc.
USA

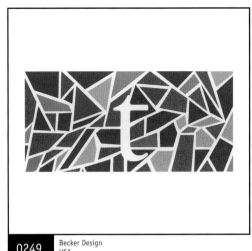

0249 Becker Design
USA

0250 Becker Design
USA

0251 Studio Boot
The Netherlands

0252 IE Design + Communications
USA

0253 Voice Design
USA

0254 Splash Interactive Limited
Canada

0255 Splash Interactive Limited
USA

0256   Muggie Ramadani Design Studio
Denmark

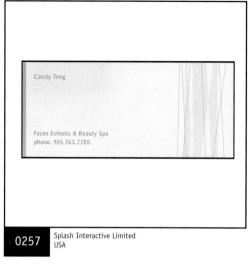

0257   Splash Interactive Limited
USA

0258   Splash Interactive Limited
USA

0259   Loewy
UK

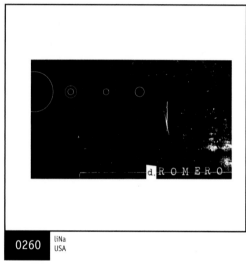

0260   liNa
USA

0261   liNa
USA

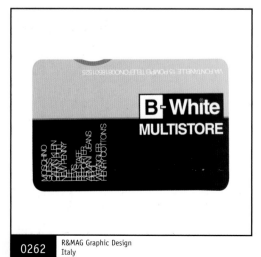

0262   R&MAG Graphic Design
Italy

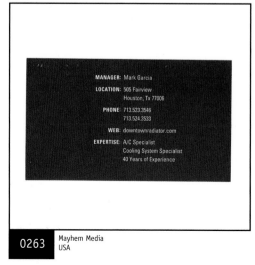

0263   Mayhem Media
USA

0264   Mayhem Media
USA

Lloyds Graphic Design
New Zealand

0266 Design Ranch
USA

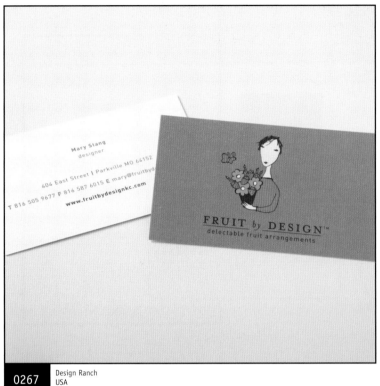

| 0267 | Design Ranch USA |

| 0268 | Design Ranch USA |

| 0269 | Huss | Büro für creative Massnahmen Germany |

| 0270 | Huss | Büro für creative Massnahmen Germany |

| 0271 | Landini Associates
Australia |

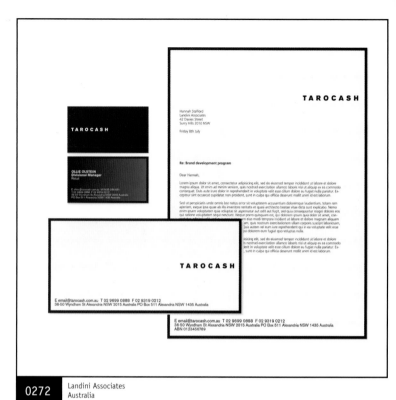

| 0272 | Landini Associates
Australia |

| 0273 | Nocturnal Graphic Design Studio
USA |

| 0274 | Aloof Design
UK |

TRUEFACES CREATION SDN BHD
21, Jalan USJ 9/5P, Subang Business Centre
47620 UEP Subang Jaya
Selangor Darul Ehsan, Malaysia
tel : +6 03 8023 2121
fax: +6 03 8023 0021
website: www.truefaces.com.my

an expression of emotions
through art **trueFACES**™
by allentan

@llentan
mobile +6 012 208 2608
allentan@truefaces.com.my

TrueFACES paintings are also displayed
@ KIARA-COM SDN BHD
Suite A-0G-03, Block A, Plaza Mont Kiara
2, Jalan Kiara, Mont Kiara, 50480 Kuala Lumpur

Canon

@llentan
mobile +6 012 208 2608
allentan@truefaces.com.my

TrueFACES paintings are also displayed
@ KIARA-COM SDN BHD
Suite A-0G-03, Block A, Plaza Mont Kiara
2, Jalan Kiara, Mont Kiara, 50480 Kuala Lumpur

Canon

@llentan
mobile +6 012 208 2608
allentan@truefaces.com.my

TrueFACES paintings are also displayed
@ KIARA-COM SDN BHD
Suite A-0G-03, Block A, Plaza Mont Kiara
2, Jalan Kiara, Mont Kiara, 50480 Kuala Lumpur

Canon

@llentan
mobile +6 012 208 2608
allentan@truefaces.com.my

TrueFACES paintings are also displayed
@ KIARA-COM SDN BHD
Suite A-0G-03, Block A, Plaza Mont Kiara
2, Jalan Kiara, Mont Kiara, 50480 Kuala Lumpur

Canon

@llentan
mobile +6 012 208 2608
allentan@truefaces.com.my

TrueFACES paintings are also displayed
@ KIARA-COM SDN BHD
Suite A-0G-03, Block A, Plaza Mont Kiara
2, Jalan Kiara, Mont Kiara, 50480 Kuala Lumpur

Canon

@llentan
mobile +6 012 208 2608
allentan@truefaces.com.my

TrueFACES paintings are also displayed
@ KIARA-COM SDN BHD
Suite A-0G-03, Block A, Plaza Mont Kiara
2, Jalan Kiara, Mont Kiara, 50480 Kuala Lumpur

Canon

@llentan
mobile +6 012 208 2608
allentan@truefaces.com.my

TrueFACES paintings are also displayed
@ KIARA-COM SDN BHD
Suite A-0G-03, Block A, Plaza Mont Kiara
2, Jalan Kiara, Mont Kiara, 50480 Kuala Lumpur

Canon

@llentan
mobile +6 012 208 2608
allentan@truefaces.com.my

TrueFACES paintings are also displayed
@ KIARA-COM SDN BHD
Suite A-0G-03, Block A, Plaza Mont Kiara
2, Jalan Kiara, Mont Kiara, 50480 Kuala Lumpur

Canon

0277 Gardner Design
USA

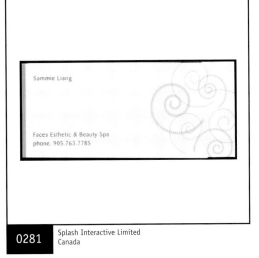

0278 Gardner Design
USA

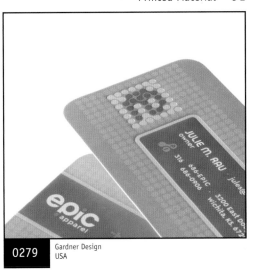

0279 Gardner Design
USA

0280 Trickett & Webb Ltd.
UK

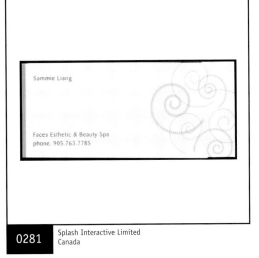

0281 Splash Interactive Limited
Canada

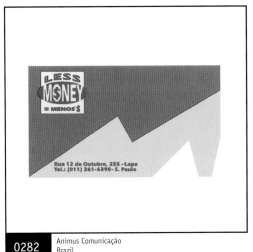

0282 Animus Comunicação
Brazil

0283 Animus Comunicação
Brazil

0284 Visible Ink
USA

0285 Jeff Labbé Design 0950
USA

0286   Greteman Group
USA

0287   LG Productions
USA

0288   Roger Gefvert Designs
USA

0289   Jon Nedry
USA

0290   Bartels & Company, Inc.
USA

0291   Apple Graphics & Advertising of Merrick, Inc.
USA

0292   Duck Soup Graphics, Inc.
Canada

0293   Phoenix Creative
USA

0294   Alison Goudreault, Inc.
USA

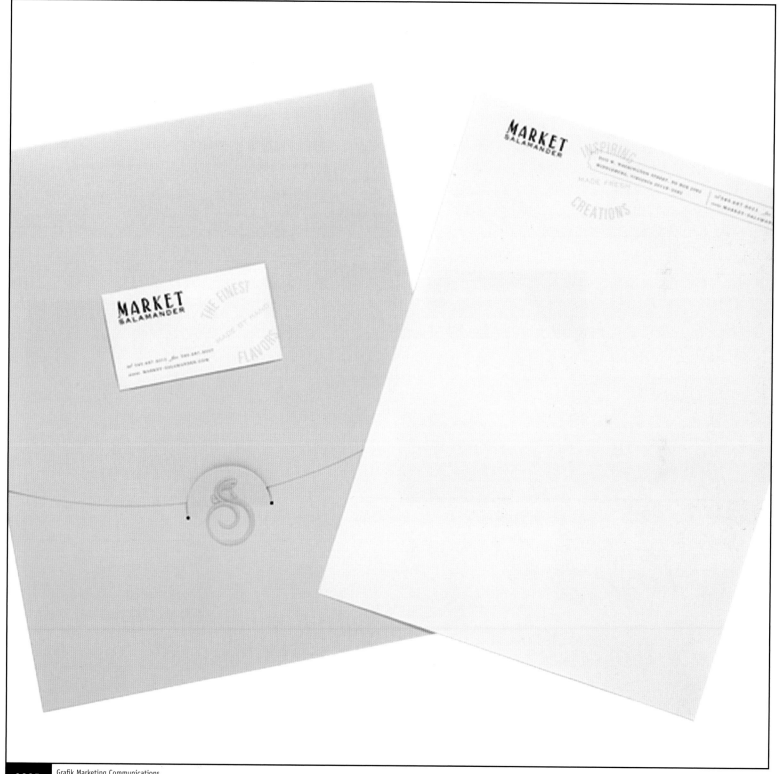

0297   fFurious
Singapore

0298   Unreal
UK

0299   Muggie Ramadani Design Studio
Denmark

0300   Templin Brink Design
USA

 0301   Gardner Design
USA

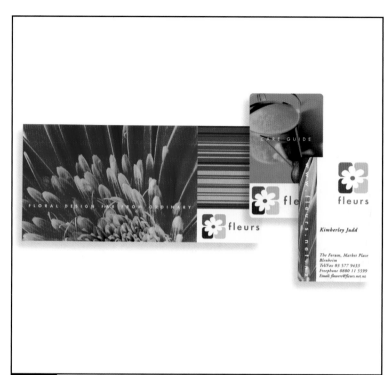

0302   Lloyds Graphic Design
New Zealand

0303   Whitney Edwards LLC
USA

0304   Whitney Edwards LLC
USA

0307 MiresBall
USA

0308 Kirby Stephens Design, Inc.
USA

0309 Kirby Stephens Design, Inc.
USA

0310 The Design Company
USA

0311 The Design Company
USA

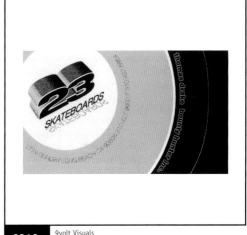

0312 9volt Visuals
USA

0313 Widmeyer Design
USA

0314 Widmeyer Design
USA

0315 Design Center
USA

AVONLEA FLORAL ARTS

NICOLE KRAMER

FOSHAY TOWER
106 SOUTH 9TH STREET
MINNEAPOLIS, MN 55402
TELEPHONE (612) 359-9119
FACSIMILE 359-9131

0316 Design Center
USA

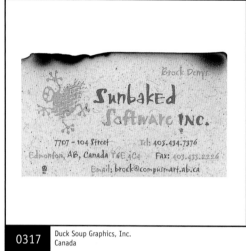

0317 Duck Soup Graphics, Inc.
Canada

MARTIN
CROWDER
H A I R   S A L O N

MARTIN CROWDER

0318 Sayles Graphic Design
USA

5709 HICKMAN ROAD
DES MOINES, IOWA 50310
515-277-1709

YOUR APPOINTMENT IS:

0319 Sayles Graphic Design
USA

0320 Greteman Group
USA

A
SHOW
OF
HANDS
FULL SERVICE SALON

AMANI
owner/nail artist

408.371.8877

2160 S. Bascom Ave. Campbell, California
9 5 0 0 8

0321 Jill Morrison Design
USA

CLOTIA
WOOD & METAL WORKS, INC.

BERT CLOTHIER

536 S. COMMERCE
WICHITA, KS 67202
T 316-263-9722
F 316-263-1042

0322 Insight Design Communication
USA

FURNITURE
·OPTIONS

Barney Lehnher

0323 Greteman Group
USA

in
innovative products for living
eric read . . . . principal
825 san anselmo ave
san anselmo ca USA 94960
fone 415.456.4175

inhaus Industries

0324 Brand Engine
USA

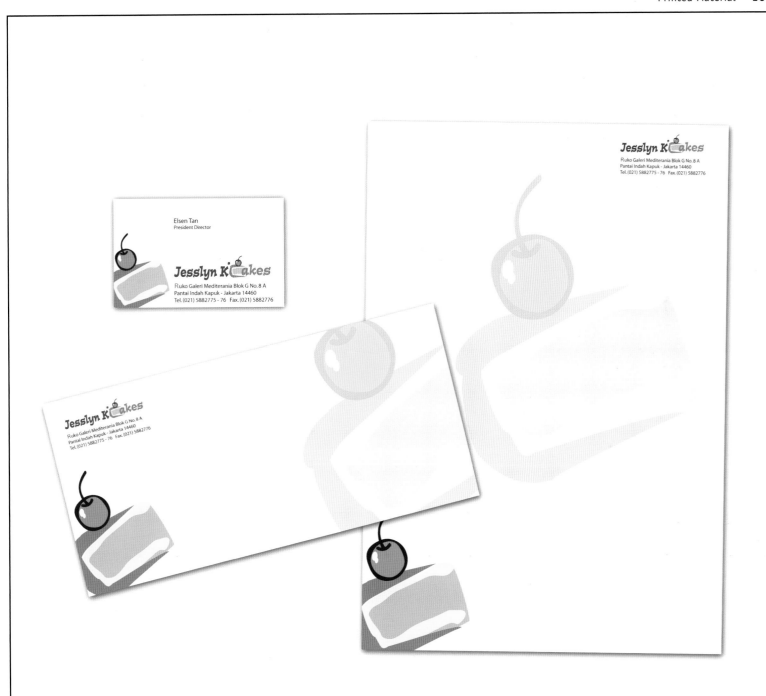

suna at home
93 main street
andover, ma 01810

suna
at home

Grand Opening in Andover
Saturday, February 12th, 10–5pm

20% discount all day! Come celebrate the opening of
Andover's new home furnishings and accessories store.

furniture | rugs | lamps | pillows | mirrors | candles | gifts

93 Main Street (Be

suna
at home

Grand Opening in And
Saturday, February 12th, 10

lynn alexander

furnishings • accessories • gifts

93 main street, andover ma 01810
phone/fax 978.475.0091

0327 Aloof Design
UK

0328 Nothing: Something: NY
USA

0329 Greenmelon Inc.
Canada

0330 Gouthier Design
USA

0331 · Gouthier Design · USA

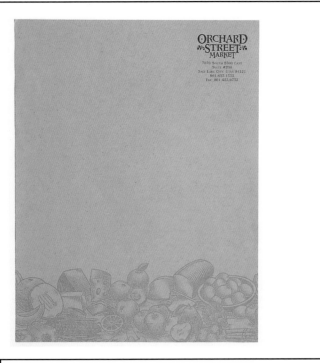

0332 · Love Communications · USA

0333 · Design Ranch · USA

0334 · Design Ranch · USA

MEREDITH KAHN
|| WWW.MADEHERTHINK.COM ||
merikahn@madeherthink.com
t. 646 || 267 || 1793 — f. 718 || 349 || 3804

Ruben Esparza Design
USA

0337 Entermotion Design Studio
USA

0338 Entermotion Design Studio
USA

For five years Bert and John Jacobs slept in their van, lived on PB&J and sold tee shirts door-to-door in college dorms. Then in 1994, with a combined sum of $78 in the bank, they created Jake and he showed them the way. Ten years later, Jake and Life is good® are spreading optimism nationwide.
www.lifeisgood.com

0339 Gardner Design
USA

0340 Gardner Design
USA

0341 Gardner Design
USA

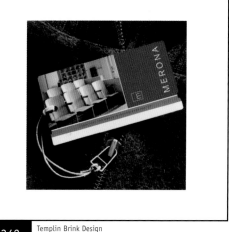

0342 Templin Brink Design
USA

0343 Mucca Design
USA

PRADA

0344 Prada
Italy

0345 Gabriel Kalach - Visual Communication
USA

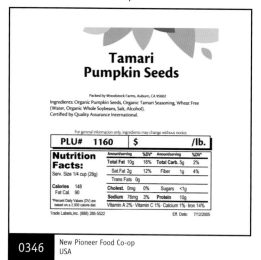

0346   New Pioneer Food Co-op
USA

0347   New Pioneer Food Co-op
USA

0348   Forum Studio Creativo
Mexico

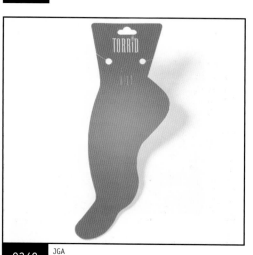

0349   JGA
USA

0350   JGA
USA

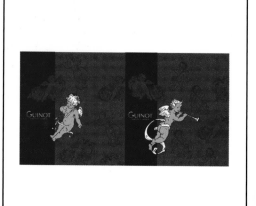

0351   JGA
USA

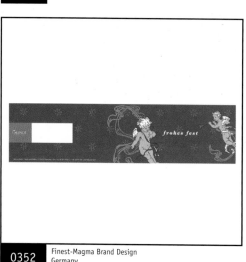

0352   Finest-Magma Brand Design
Germany

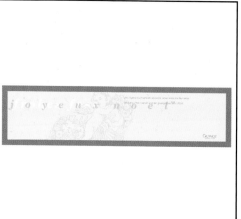

0353   Finest-Magma Brand Design
Germany

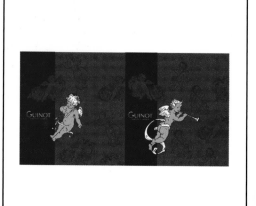

0354   Finest-Magma Brand Design
Germany

Creative Spark
UK

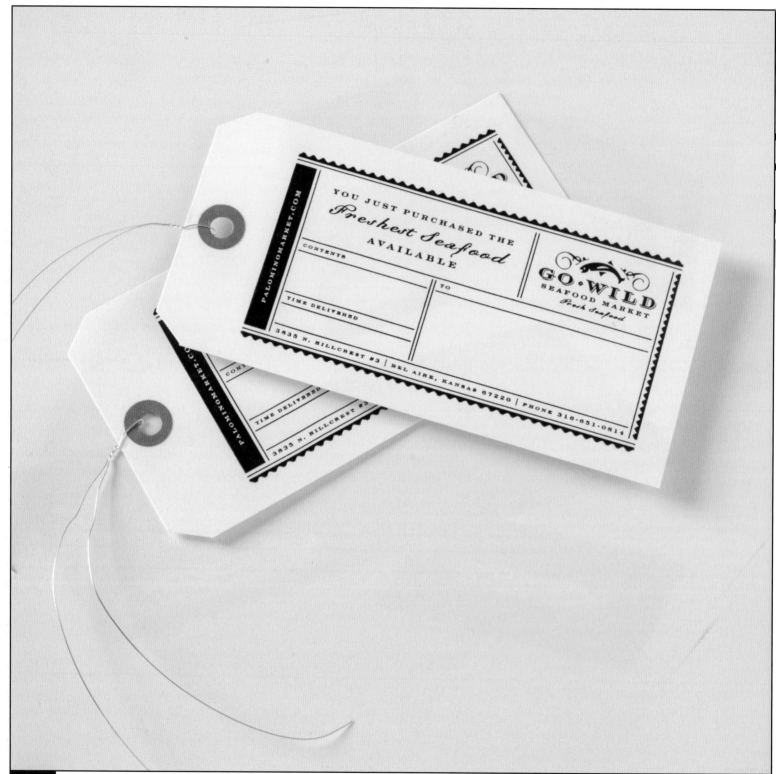

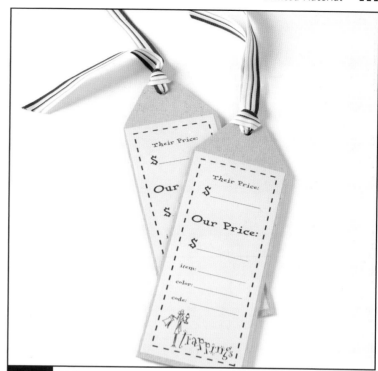

0357
Entermotion Design Studio
USA

0358
delphine
USA

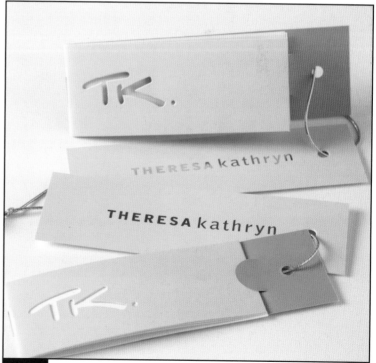

0359
delphine
USA

0360
IE Design + Communications
USA

0361	Design Ranch USA

0362	Design Ranch USA

0363	Design Ranch USA

0364	Huss	Büro für creative Massnahmen Germany

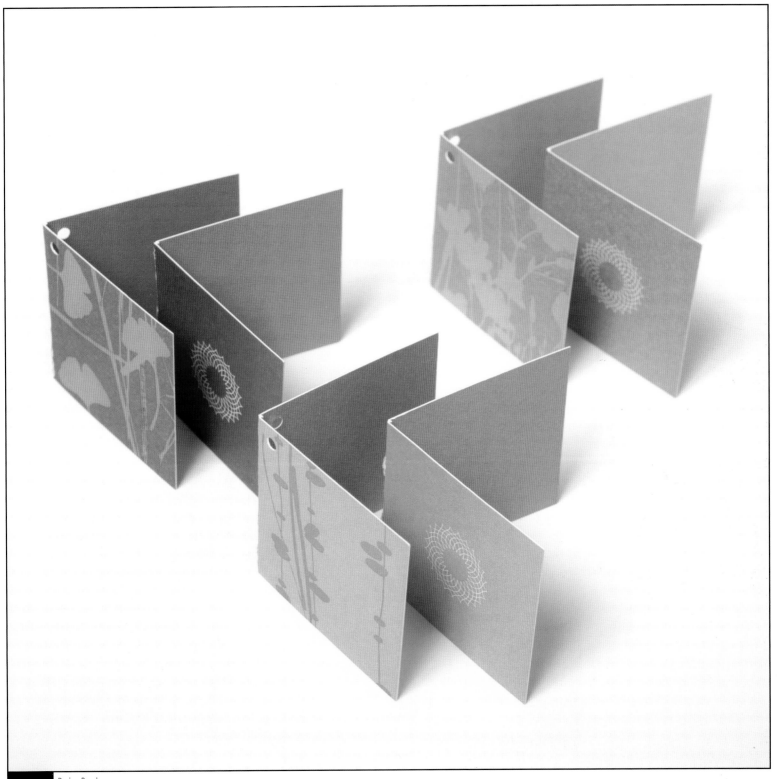

0365   Design Ranch
       USA

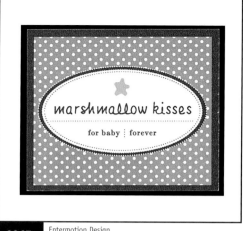

0367 · Entermotion Design · USA

0368 · Entermotion Design · USA

0369 · Entermotion Design · USA

0370 · Entermotion Design · USA

0371 · Wunderburg Design · Germany

0372 · Kinesis · USA

0373 · A. Graphic Communications (AGC) · USA

0374 · A. Graphic Communications (AGC) · USA

0375 · A. Graphic Communications (AGC) · USA

0376	A. Graphic Communications (AGC) USA
0377	A. Graphic Communications (AGC) USA
0378	A. Graphic Communications (AGC) USA

0379	Good Night TV USA
0380	Good Night TV USA
0381	Lloyds Graphic Design New Zealand

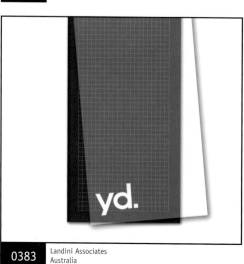

0382	Nocturnal Graphic Design Studio USA
0383	Landini Associates Australia
0384	Skaggs Design USA

Nothing: Something: NY
USA

0387 Nothing: Something: NY
USA

0388 Nothing: Something: NY
USA

0389 Aloof Design
UK

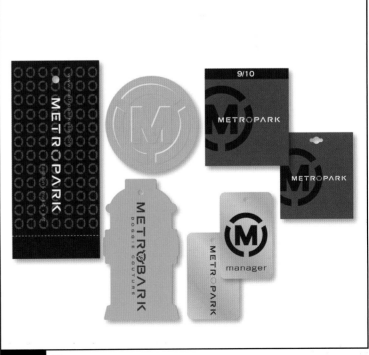

0390 JGA
USA

0391   Silvia Vallim Design
Brazil

0392   LAYFIELD
Australia

0393   Hardy Design
Brazil

0394   Hardy Design
Brazil

Worn over the shoulders our stole bandonna can be used as a shawl.

Wrap wine bottles and other small bottles.

Use it

If your feeli you can and

PenguinCube
Lebanon

| 0397 | Hardy Design
Brazil |

| 0398 | Hardy Design
Brazil |

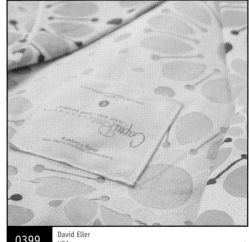

| 0399 | David Eller
USA |

| 0400 | Muggie Ramadani Design Studio
Denmark |

| 0401 | Whitney Edwards LLC
USA |

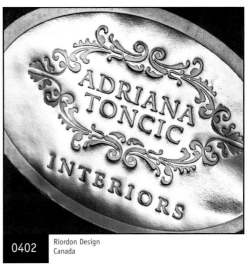

| 0402 | Riordon Design
Canada |

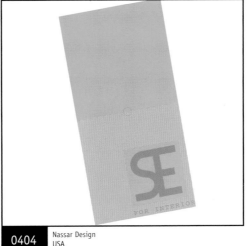

| 0403 | Lloyds Graphic Design
New Zealand |

| 0404 | Nassar Design
USA |

| 0405 | Nassar Design
USA |

| 0406 | Kinesis
USA |

| 0407 | Templin Brink Design
USA |

| 0408 | B.L.A. Design Company
USA |

| 0409 | WL2 Studios NYC
USA |

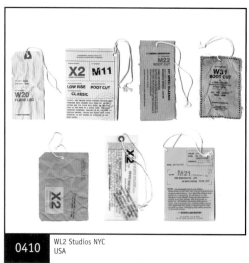

| 0410 | WL2 Studios NYC
USA |

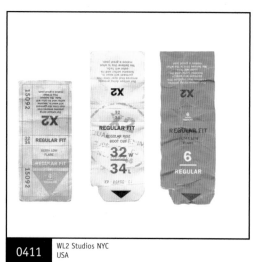

| 0411 | WL2 Studios NYC
USA |

| 0412 | WL2 Studios NYC
USA |

| 0413 | WL2 Studios NYC
USA |

| 0414 | LAYFIELD
Australia |

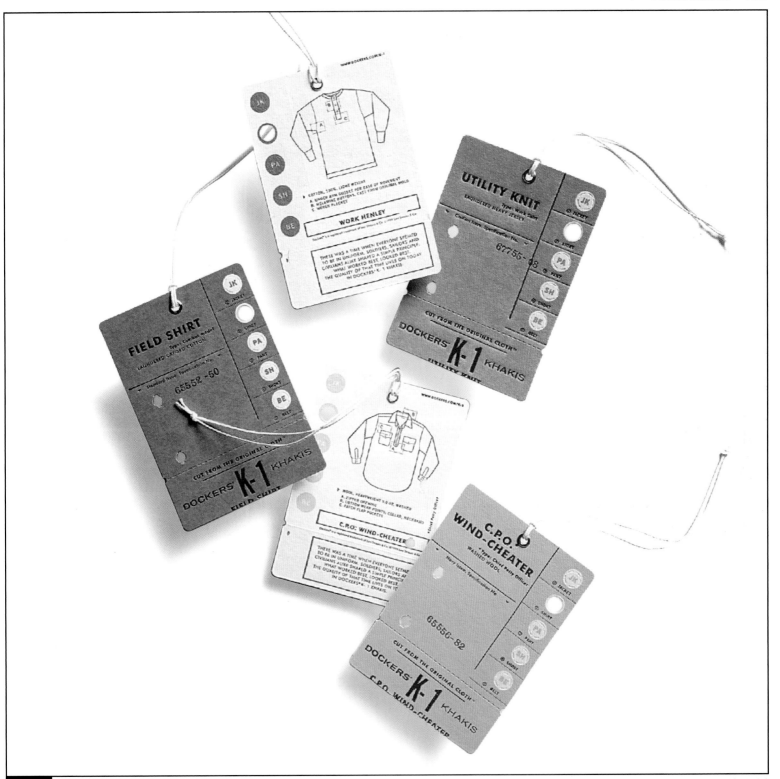

0417 Epos, Inc.
USA

0418 Graphic Culture
USA

0419 Graphic Culture
USA

0420 Graphic Culture
USA

0421   Landini Associates
         Australia

0422   Landini Associates
         Australia

0423   Wallace Church, Inc.
         USA

0424   Wallace Church, Inc.
         USA

Wallace Church, Inc.
USA

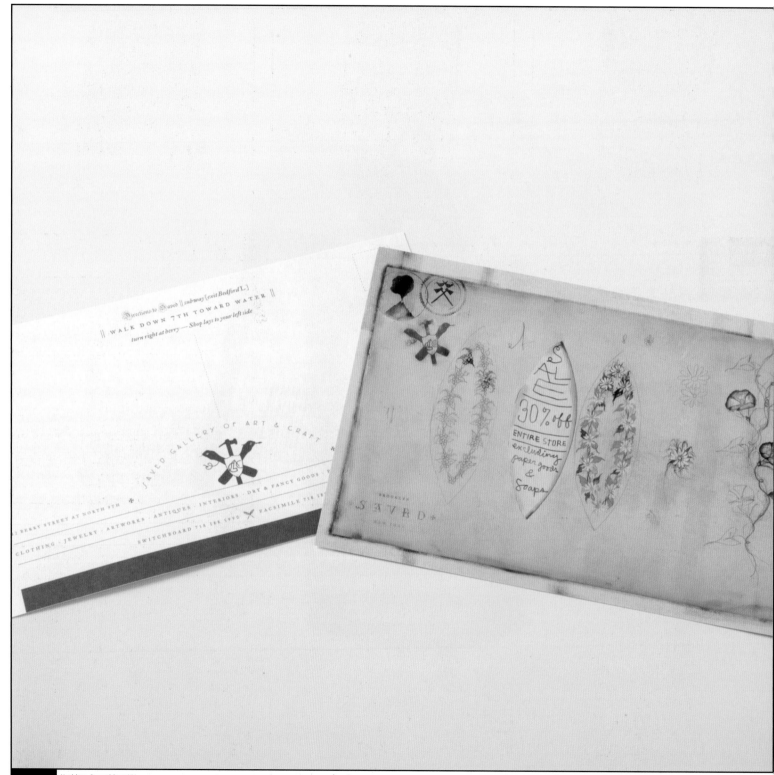

Nothing: Something: NY
USA

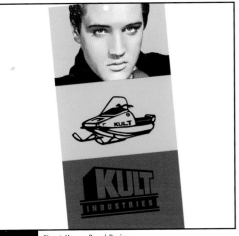

0427 — Finest-Magma Brand Design
Germany

0428 — Finest-Magma Brand Design
Germany

0429 — Finest-Magma Brand Design
Germany

0430 — Finest-Magma Brand Design
Germany

0431 — Finest-Magma Brand Design
Germany

0432 — Finest-Magma Brand Design
Germany

0433 — Finest-Magma Brand Design
Germany

0434 — Finest-Magma Brand Design
Germany

0435 — Finest-Magma Brand Design
Germany

0436 Kendall Ross Brand Development & Design
USA

0437 Entermotion Design Studio
USA

0438 Kendall Ross Brand Development & Design
USA

0439 Kendall Ross Brand Development & Design
USA

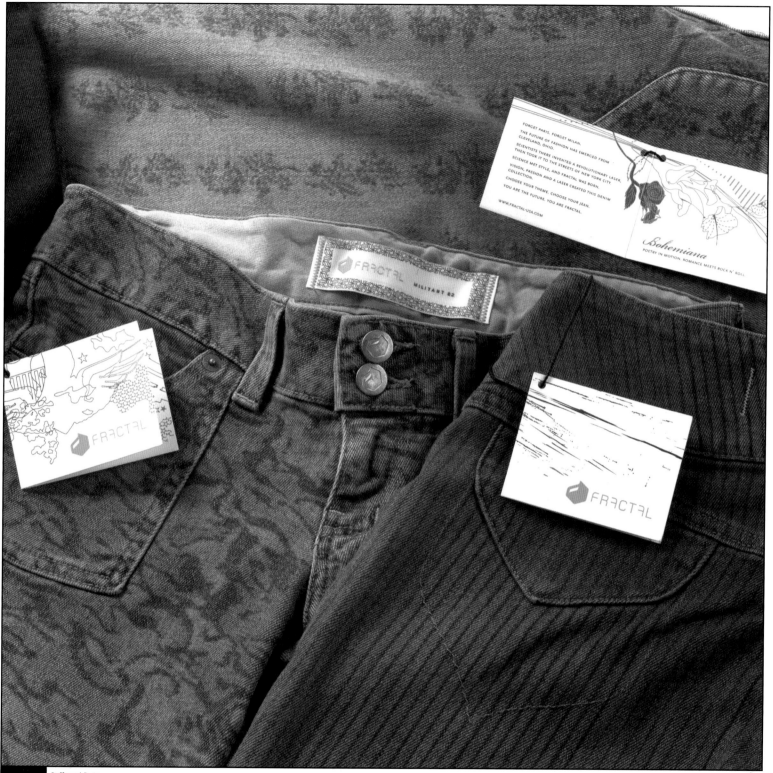

FORGET PARIS. FORGET MILAN.
THE FUTURE OF FASHION HAS EMERGED FROM
CLEVELAND, OHIO.

SCIENTISTS THERE INVENTED A REVOLUTIONARY LASER,
THEN TOOK IT TO THE STREETS OF NEW YORK CITY.

SCIENCE MET STYLE, AND FRACTAL WAS BORN.

VISION, PASSION AND A LASER CREATED THIS DENIM
COLLECTION.

CHOOSE YOUR THEME. CHOOSE YOUR JEAN.
YOU ARE THE FUTURE. YOU ARE FRACTAL.

WWW.FRACTAL-USA.COM

Bohemiana
POETRY IN MOTION. ROMANCE MEETS ROCK N' ROLL.

Duffy and Partners
USA

essenciale.

av contorno, 8847 bhz tel 3335.6678

www.e-essenciale.com.br

0441

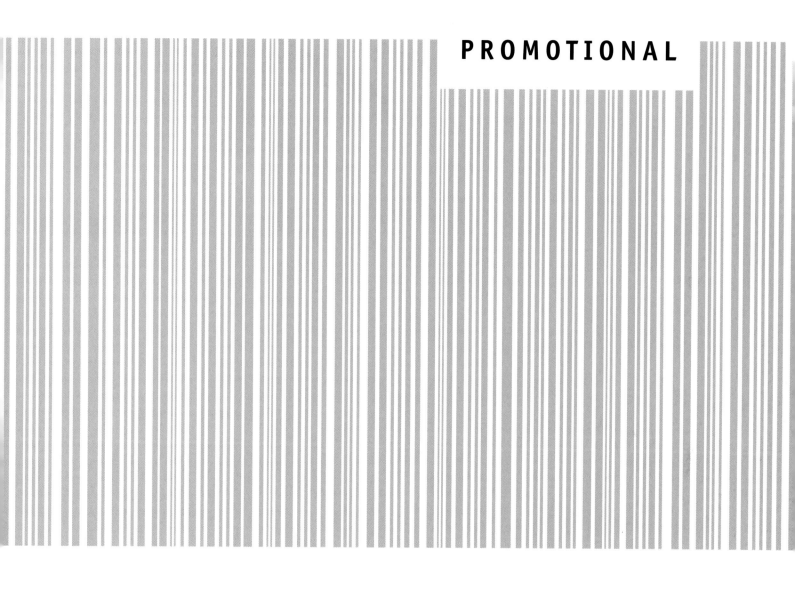

PROMOTIONAL

0 5 4 0

an evening with **kate lane** featuring

james perse

Thursday, August 11 from 6pm - 9pm at kate lane

0441 Entermotion Design Studio
USA

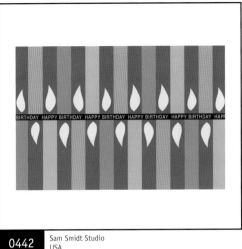

| 0442 | Sam Smidt Studio
USA |

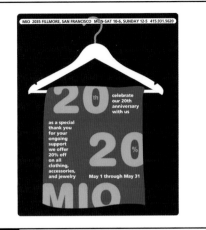

| 0443 | Sam Smidt Studio
USA |

| 0444 | Tom Fowler Inc.
USA |

| 0445 | Plazm
USA |

| 0446 | Plazm
USA |

| 0447 | Plazm
USA |

| 0448 | Plazm
USA |

| 0449 | Plazm
USA |

| 0450 | Plazm
USA |

0451 Sayles Graphic Design
USA

0452 Kendall Ross Brand Development & Design
USA

0453 Kendall Ross Brand Development & Design
USA

0454 Kendall Ross Brand Development & Design
USA

0455 Kendall Ross Brand Development & Design
USA

0456 Kendall Ross Brand Development & Design
USA

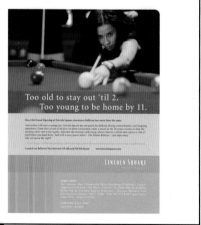

0457 Kendall Ross Brand Development & Design
USA

0458 Kendall Ross Brand Development & Design
USA

0459 Riordon Design
Canada

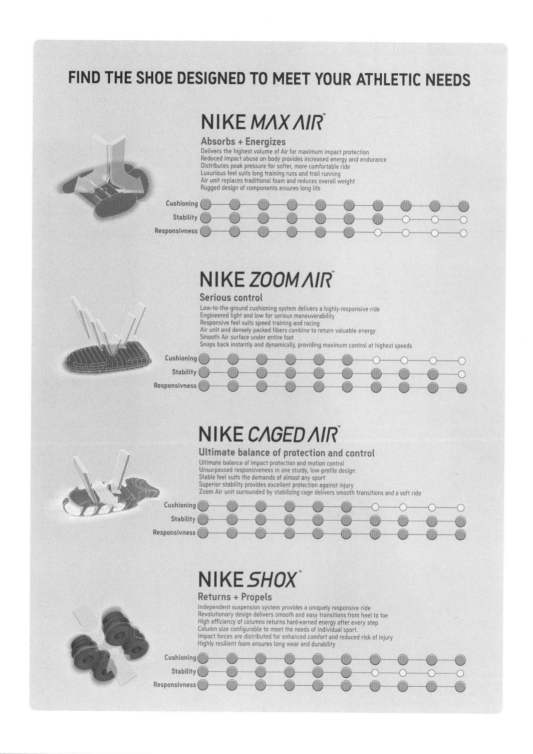

FIND THE SHOE DESIGNED TO MEET YOUR ATHLETIC NEEDS

NIKE MAX AIR

Absorbs + Energizes

Delivers the highest volume of Air for maximum impact protection
Reduced impact abuse on body provides increased energy and endurance
Distributes peak pressure for softer, more comfortable ride
Luxurious feel suits long training runs and trail running
Air unit replaces traditional foam and reduces overall weight
Rugged design of components ensures long life

Cushioning
Stability
Responsivness

NIKE ZOOM AIR

Serious control

Low-to-the-ground cushioning system delivers a highly-responsive ride
Engineered light and low for serious maneuverability
Responsive feel suits speed training and racing
Air unit and densely packed fibers combine to return valuable energy
Smooth Air surface under entire foot
Snaps back instantly and dynamically, providing maximum control at highest speeds

Cushioning
Stability
Responsivness

NIKE CAGED AIR

Ultimate balance of protection and control

Ultimate balance of impact protection and motion control
Unsurpassed responsiveness in one sturdy, low-profile design
Stable feel suits the demands of almost any sport
Superior stability provides excellent protection against injury
Zoom Air unit surrounded by stabilizing cage delivers smooth transitions and a soft ride

Cushioning
Stability
Responsivness

NIKE SHOX

Returns + Propels

Independent suspension system provides a uniquely responsive ride
Revolutionary design delivers smooth and easy transitions from heel to toe
High efficiency of columns returns hard-earned energy after every step
Column size configurable to meet the needs of individual sport.
Impact forces are distributed for enhanced comfort and reduced risk of injury
Highly resilient foam ensures long wear and durability

Cushioning
Stability
Responsivness

Hosted By:

Nicky Hilton

Appearances By:

Carmen Electra

Mya

Cast Members Of MTV's Laguna Beach

Music By:

DJ Whoo Kid
G-Unit Radio
On Shade 45
live on Sirius Radio

DJ AM

DJ Reach

Black Violins

NEXT

BEAUTY IS ONLY SKIN DEEP,
BUT STYLE IS IN THE JEANS.

Please Be Our Guest
At The Fashion
Event Of The Year

0462 Lloyds Graphic Design
New Zealand

0463 Nocturnal Graphic Design Studio
USA

0464 Nocturnal Graphic Design Studio
USA

0465 Hardy Design
Brazil

0466 Hardy Design
Brazil

0467 Hardy Design
Brazil

0468 Hardy Design
Brazil

0469 Hardy Design
Brazil

BROADCASTING TO MEMBERS

NEWS

The BULL

CDWAREHOUSE

Greenmelon Inc
Canada

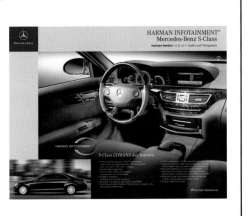

0472 Mars Advertising
USA

0473 Mars Advertising
USA

0474 Muggie Ramadani Design Studio
Denmark

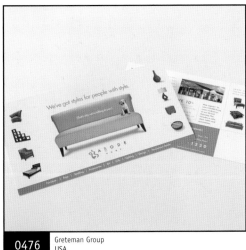

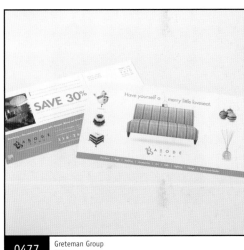

0475 Greteman Group
USA

0476 Greteman Group
USA

0477 Greteman Group
USA

0478 Muggie Ramadani Design Studio
Denmark

0479 Muggie Ramadani Design Studio
Denmark

0480 Muggie Ramadani Design Studio
Denmark

0481   Hollis Brand Communications
USA

0482   Hollis Brand Communications
USA

0483   Hollis Brand Communications
USA

0484   Hollis Brand Communications
USA

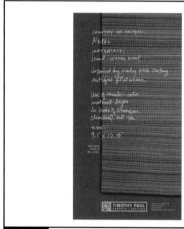

0485   Design Nut, LLC
USA

0486   Design Nut, LLC
USA

0487   JGA
USA

0488   JGA
USA

0489   R&MAG Graphic Design
Italy

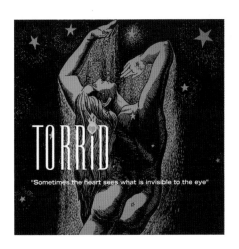

"Sometimes the heart sees what is invisible to the eye"

"Absence is to love what wind is to fire; it extinguishes the small, it enkindles the great."

Comte DeBussey-Rubutin

A Love that became so strong and all encompassing that it became an addiction

0492 New Pioneer Food Co-op
USA

0493 New Pioneer Food Co-op
USA

0494 Kinesis
USA

0495 Ellen Bruss Design
USA

0496   Entermotion Design Studio
USA

0497   Entermotion Design Studio
USA

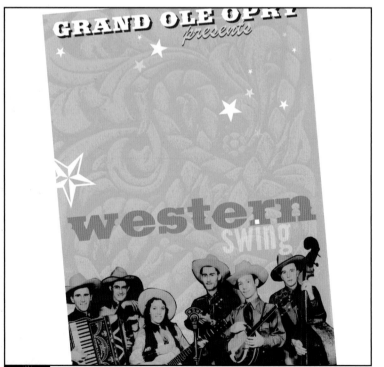

0498   Kiku Obata + Company
USA

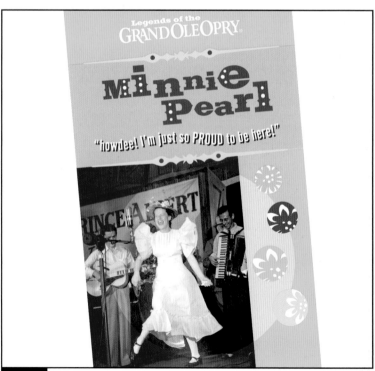

0499   Kiku Obata + Company
USA

MURRAY MOTOR IMPORTS
COLORADO'S MERCEDES-BENZ AND BMW DEALERSHIP

THANK YOU.

IN APPRECIATION OF YOUR GENEROSITY AND
SERVICE TO THE DENVER COMMUNITY, PLEASE
ACCEPT THIS VALET PARKING PASS FROM
MURRAY MOTOR IMPORTS AND CHERRY CREEK.

CHERRY CREEK SHOPPING CENTER
MANAGEMENT OFFICE
3000 E. FIRST AVENUE
DENVER, CO 80205

CLUB CHERRY CREEK

MURRAY MOTOR IMPORTS

CLUB CHERRY CREEK
GIVING TO THOSE WHO GIVE TO THE COMMUNITY

A GIFT FROM MURRAY
MOTOR IMPORTS

Purchase a new Mercedes-Benz or BMW vehicle
from Murray Motor Imports and you will receive a
gift from our boutique.

Limit one per person, while supplies last,
may be discontinued at any time.

COMPLIMENTARY CHERRY
CREEK PEN OR TOTE BAG

Present this coupon at the guest services booth on
the lower level of the Cherry Creek Shopping Center
to receive your complimentary pen or tote bag.

Limit one per person, while supplies last.

Ellen Bruss Design
USA

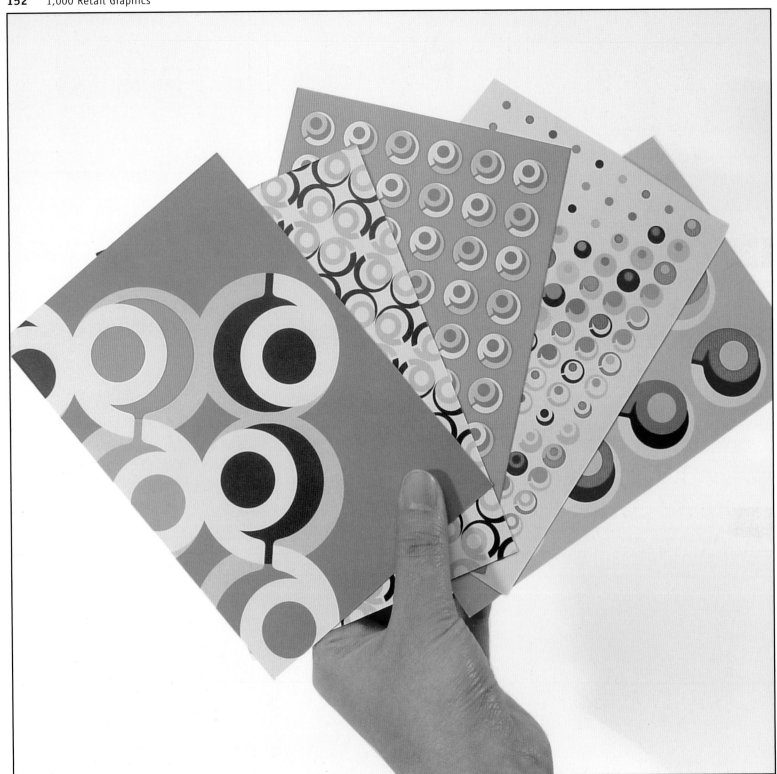

Desgrippes Gobé
USA

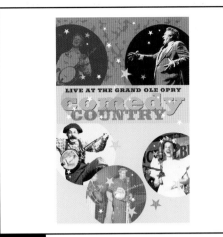

0502	Kiku Obata + Company USA

0503	Kiku Obata + Company USA

0504	Gabriel Kalach - Visual Communication USA

0505	Gabriel Kalach - Visual Communication USA

0506	Gabriel Kalach - Visual Communication USA

0507	Diesel USA

0508	Diesel USA

0509	Diesel USA

0510	Hermès France

0511	Hermès France

0512	Kinetic Singapore Singapore

0513	Design Bridge Ltd. UK

0514	Design Bridge Ltd. UK

0515	AdamsMorioka USA

0516	Brandhouse WTS UK

0517	Love Communications USA

0518	Love Communications USA

0519	Love Communications USA

0522   Lemley Design
USA

0523   Lemley Design
USA

0524   Lemley Design
USA

0525   Lemley Design
USA

0526   Lemley Design
USA

0527   Coach
USA

0528   Coach
USA

0529   Gardner Design
USA

COACH

..LY SOLOMON SOHO ARTS PIONEER

HOLLY'S COACH BAG № 9027

1-800-262-2411 COACH ERGO MINI SATCHEL

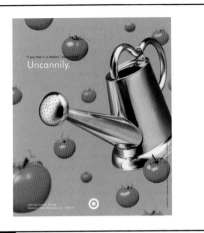

0532 Templin Brink Design
USA

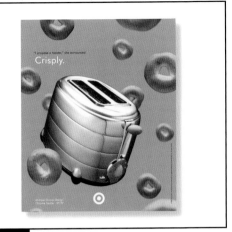

0533 Templin Brink Design
USA

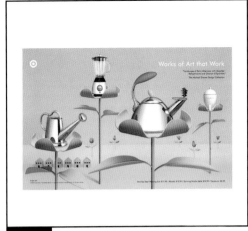

0534 Templin Brink Design
USA

0535 Templin Brink Design
USA

0536 Gardner Design
USA

0537 Gardner Design
USA

0538 Gardner Design
USA

0539 Gardner Design
USA

0540 Grafik Marketing Communications
USA

0571
TrueFaces Creation Snd Bhd
West Malaysia

0541

PACKAGING

0541   Hornall Anderson Design Works
USA

Hornall Anderson Design Works
USA

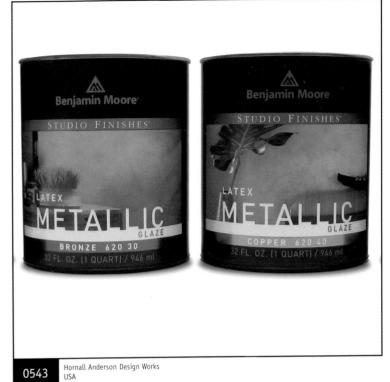

Hornall Anderson Design Works
USA

Hornall Anderson Design Works
USA

Hornall Anderson Design Works
USA

0546   Sayles Graphic Design
USA

0547   Landini Associates
Australia

0548   Arcadia Studio
USA

0549   Arcadia Studio
USA

Greenmelon Inc.
Canada

Le Chateau Marketing + Design Team
Canada

0552 Arcadia Studio
USA

0553 Arcadia Studio
USA

0554 Arcadia Studio
USA

0555 Lloyds Graphic Design
New Zealand

0556 Greenmelon Inc.
Canada

0557 Greenmelon Inc.
Canada

0558 Ideas Frescas (Fresh Ideas)
El Salvador

0559 Miriello Grafico
USA

0560 Miriello Grafico
USA

0561 Finest-Magma Brand Design
Germany

0562 JGA
USA

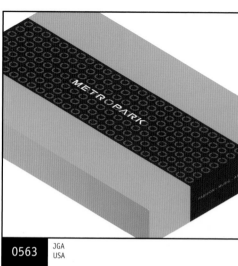

0563 JGA
USA

0564 JGA
USA

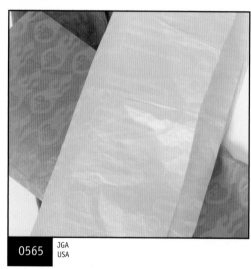

0565 JGA
USA

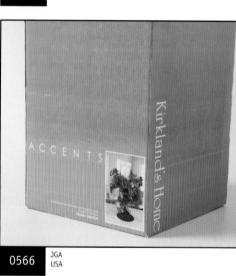

0566 JGA
USA

0567 JGA
USA

0568 JGA
USA

0569 TrueFaces Creation Sdn Bhd
West Malaysia

0572 Lloyds Graphic Design
New Zealand

0573 LAYFIELD
Australia

0574 Hardy Design
Brazil

0575 R&MAG Graphic Design
Italy

0576 Lemley Design
USA

0577 Matcha Design
USA

0578 Lemley Design
USA

0579 Lemley Design
USA

TULLY'S COFFEE

DISCOVER

HOLIDAY

WITH US

TRADITIONAL

MULLING

SPICES

A tantalizing combination of lemon, orange, cinnamon, cranberry, vanilla and spices.

NET WT. 4oz. (200g)

0580   Lemley Design
USA

Ellen Bruss Design
USA

0582 Helena Seo Design
USA

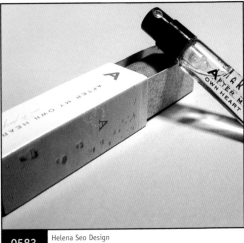

0583 Helena Seo Design
USA

0584 Helena Seo Design
USA

0585 Helena Seo Design
USA

0586 Helena Seo Design
USA

0587 Helena Seo Design
USA

0588 Ellen Bruss Design
USA

0589 Hornall Anderson Design Works
USA

0590 Hornall Anderson Design Works
USA

0591 Hornall Anderson Design Works
USA

0592 Hornall Anderson Design Works
USA

0593 Hornall Anderson Design Works
USA

0594 Prada
Italy

0595 Visionare
USA

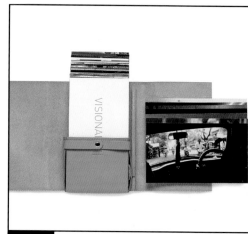

0596 Visionare
USA

0597 Parham Santana
USA

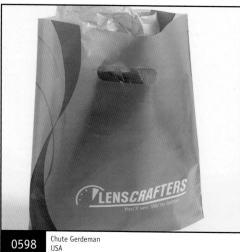

0598 Chute Gerdeman
USA

0599 Chute Gerdeman
USA

Kate Spade
USA

Lemley Design
USA

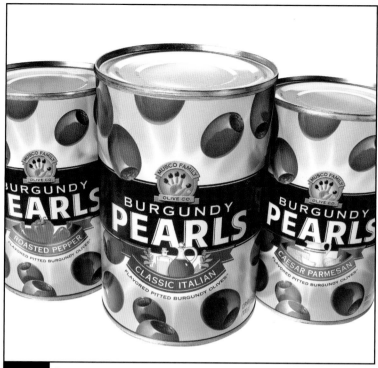

0602 Tesser
USA

0603 Courtesy of Iron Design (designer unknown)
USA

0604 Love Communications
USA

0605 Dotzero Design
USA

0606 88 Phases
USA

0607 Shiseido
USA

0608 Duffy and Partners
USA

0609 Hermès
France

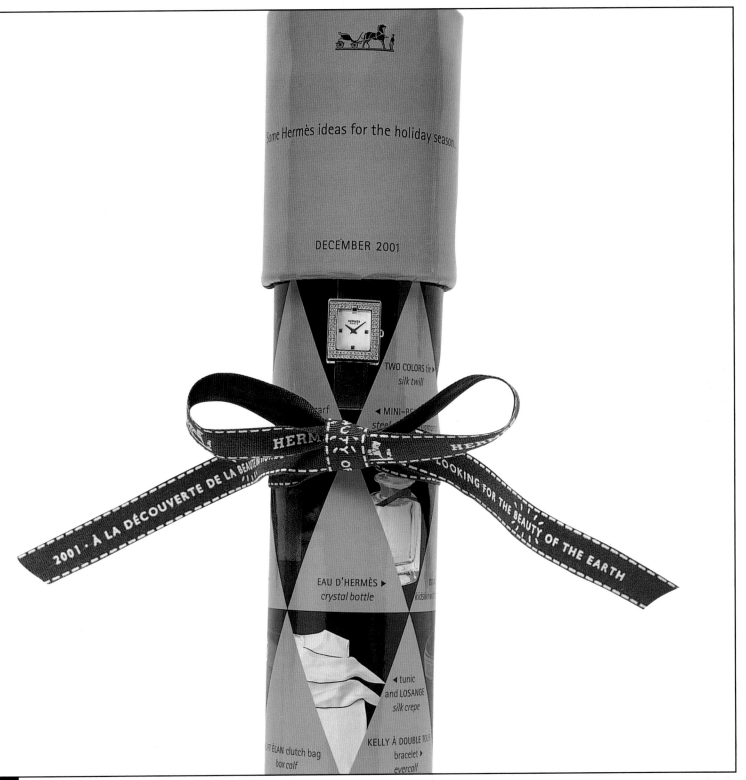

Some Hermès ideas for the holiday season...

DECEMBER 2001

TWO COLORS tie ▶
silk twill

◀ MINI-BE
scarf   steel

HERM
2001 · À LA DÉCOUVERTE DE LA BEAUTÉ   LOOKING FOR THE BEAUTY OF THE EARTH   HER

EAU D'HERMÈS ▶
crystal bottle

Di
kidskin

◀ tunic
and LOSANGE
silk crepe

KELLY À DOUBLE TOU
bracelet ▶
evercalf

FT ÉLAN clutch bag
box calf

Hermès, Thomas Pink, Kate Spade, Marc Jacobs, Michael Kors
France, UK, USA, USA, USA

0612 Chute Gerdeman
USA

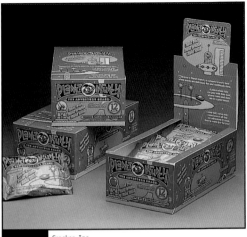

0613 Crocker, Inc.
USA

0614 Templin Brink Design
USA

0615 BC Design
USA

0616 Gateway
USA

0617 Krispy Kreme Doughnuts, Inc.
USA

0618 Grafik Marketing Communications
USA

0619 Grafik Marketing Communications
USA

0620 Morla Design
USA

0621
Wink
USA

0622
Gardner Design
USA

0623
Gardner Design
USA

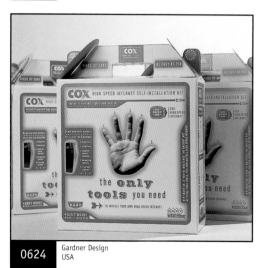

0624
Gardner Design
USA

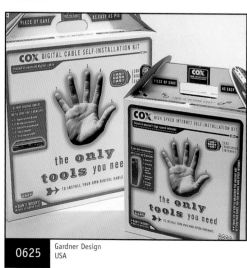

0625
Gardner Design
USA

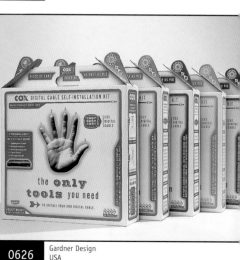

0626
Gardner Design
USA

0627
Gardner Design
USA

0628
Gardner Design
USA

0629
Gardner Design
USA

Greenmelon Inc.
Canada

0632 Fitch
USA

0633 Fitch
USA

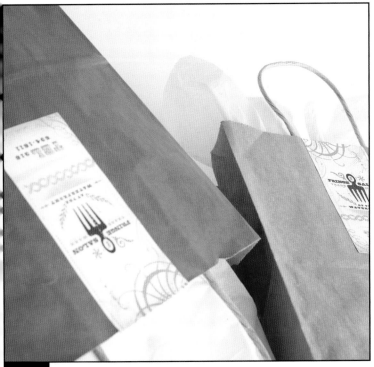

0634 Gardner Design
USA

0635 Vivitiv
USA

0636 Forum Studio Creativo
Mexico

0637 Greenmelon Inc.
Canada

0638 Turnstyle
USA

0639 Gee + Chung Design
USA

Nocturnal Graphic Design Studio
USA

0642 Gardner Design
USA

0643 Gardner Design
USA

0644 Gardner Design
USA

0645 Evenson Design Group
USA

0646 chocolateTalk, LLC
USA

0647 chocolateTalk, LLC
USA

0648 Good Night TV
USA

0649 Anders Malmströmer Grafisk Design
Sweden

0650 Sayles Graphic Design
USA

0651 design hoch drei
Germany

0652 design hoch drei
Germany

0653 design hoch drei
Germany

0654 design hoch drei
Germany

0655 Landini Associates
Australia

0656 Landini Associates
Australia

0657 Landini Associates
Australia

0658 Epos, Inc.
USA

0659 Epos, Inc.
USA

0660 Landini Associates
Australia

0661   Nocturnal Graphic Design Studio
USA

0662 Hollis Brand Communications
USA

0663 Clark Design
USA

0664 Evenson Design Group
USA

0665 Sayles Graphic Design
USA

0666 Muggie Ramadani Design Studio
Denmark

0667 The Partners Design Consultants
UK

0668 Hardy Design
Brazil

0669 Sayles Graphic Design
USA

0670 Hardy Design
Brazil

Aloof Design
UK

0672 Epos, Inc.
USA

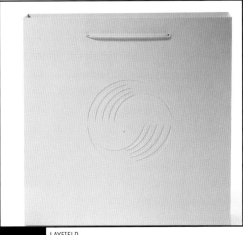

0673 LAYFIELD
Australia

0674 Finest-Magma Brand Design
Germany

0675 Finest-Magma Brand Design
Germany

0676 Finest-Magma Brand Design
Germany

0677 Finest-Magma Brand Design
Germany

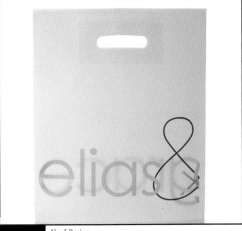

0678 Aloof Design
UK

0679 Skaggs Design
USA

0680 LAYFIELD
Australia

| 0681 | LAYFIELD
Australia |

| 0682 | chocolateTalk, LLC
USA |

| 0683 | chocolateTalk, LLC
USA |

| 0684 | chocolateTalk, LLC
USA |

| 0685 | chocolateTalk, LLC
USA |

| 0686 | chocolateTalk, LLC
USA |

| 0687 | LAYFIELD
Australia |

| 0688 | Hardy Design
Brazil |

| 0689 | Hardy Design
Brazil |

THE CHINESE PORCELAIN COMPANY

0690   Nassar Design
USA

0692   Gardner Design
        USA

0693   Gardner Design
        USA

0694   Gardner Design
        USA

0695   Gardner Design
        USA

0736
Frost Design
Australia

0696

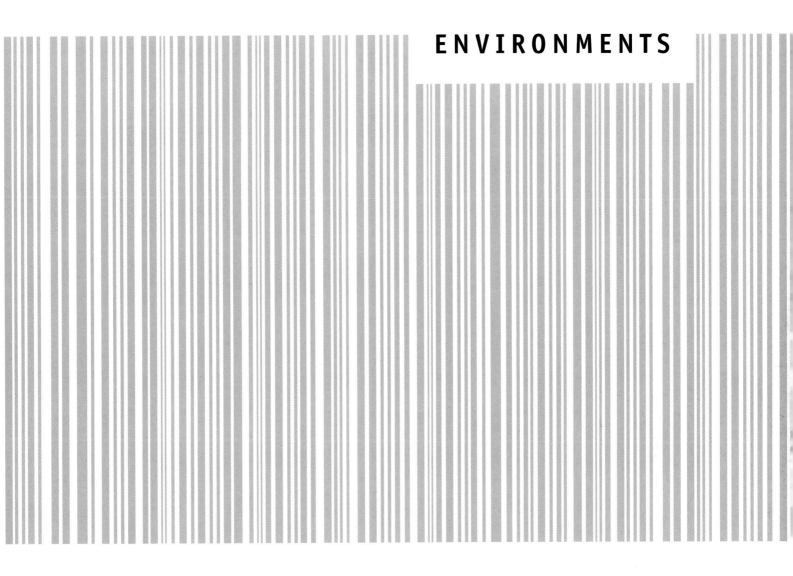

ENVIRONMENTS

0845

0696 sky design
USA

0697 sky design
USA

0698 sky design
USA

0699 sky design
USA

0700 sky design
USA

0701 Hollis Brand Communications
USA

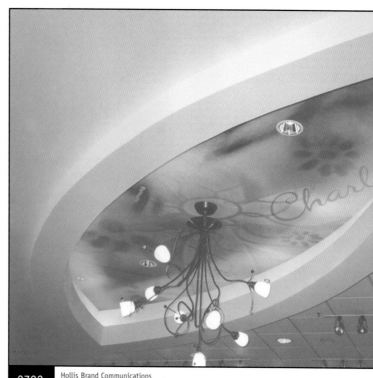

0702 Hollis Brand Communications
USA

0703 Kendall Ross Brand Development & Design
USA

0704 Hardy Design
Brazil

LINCOLN SQUARE

SHOP

The Container Store

Thomasville Home Furnishings
of Bellevue

Paper Source

Vino 100

U.S. Bank

WHERE LIFE *Meets Style*

0707 thinkDESIGNco
USA

0708 thinkDESIGNco
USA

0709 Turnstyle
USA

0710 Hollis Brand Communications
USA

0711 D/Fab
USA

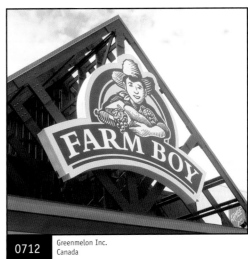
0712 Greenmelon Inc.
Canada

0713 Greteman Group
USA

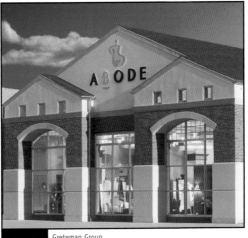
0714 Greteman Group
USA

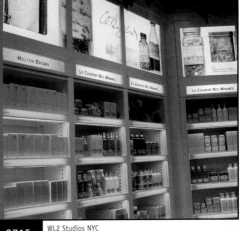
0715 WL2 Studios NYC
USA

0716 Chute Gerdeman
USA

0717 Chute Gerdeman
USA

0718 Chute Gerdeman
USA

0719 Chute Gerdeman
USA

0720 Muggie Ramadani Design Studio
Denmark

0721 Hollis Brand Communications
USA

0722 Hollis Brand Communications
USA

0723 Design Nut, LLC
USA

0724 Ideas Frescas (Fresh Ideas)
El Salvador

Landini Associates
Australia

Silvia Vallim Design
Brazil

0727   Landini Associates
Australia

0728   Landini Associates
Australia

0729   Landini Associates
Australia

0730   Landini Associates
Australia

0731 · Chute Gerdeman
USA

0732 · Chute Gerdeman
USA

0733 · Chute Gerdeman
USA

0734 · Chute Gerdeman
USA

Chute Gerdeman
USA

| 0737 | Mode
UK |

| 0738 | JGA
USA |

| 0739 | JGA
USA |

| 0740 | R&MAG Graphic Design
Italy |

| 0741 | R&MAG Graphic Design
Italy |

| 0742 | R&MAG Graphic Design
Italy |

| 0743 | R&MAG Graphic Design
Italy |

| 0744 | Desgrippes Gobé
USA |

| 0745 | Desgrippes Gobé
USA |

0746 Jack Spade
USA

0747 R by 45rpm
USA

0748 Rem Koolhaas / OMA
The Netherlands

HELMUT LANG PARFUMS

WWW.HELMUTLANG.COM

0749 Helmut Lang Parfums
USA

0750 Helmut Lang Parfums
USA

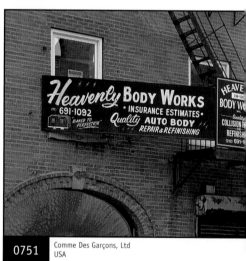

0751 Comme Des Garçons, Ltd
USA

0752 Colette
France

0753 Colette
France

0754 TrueFaces Creation Sdn Bhd
West Malaysia

TrueFaces Creation Sdn Bhd
West Malaysia

0757 JGA
USA

0758 JGA
USA

0759 JGA
USA

0760 JGA
USA

0761 JGA
USA

0762 JGA
USA

0763 JGA
USA

0764 JGA
USA

JGA
USA

Fitch
USA

0767   JGA
USA

0768   JGA
USA

0769   Fitch
USA

0770   Fitch
USA

0771   Fitch
USA

0772   JGA
USA

0773   Gateway
USA

0774   Krispy Kreme Doughnuts, Inc.
USA

0775   Krispy Kreme Doughnuts, Inc.
USA

0776 Kanner Architects
USA

0777 Kanner Architects
USA

0778 Kanner Architects
USA

0779 Kanner Architects
USA

0780 Kanner Architects
USA

0781 Kanner Architects
USA

0782 Kanner Architects
USA

0783 Kanner Architects
USA

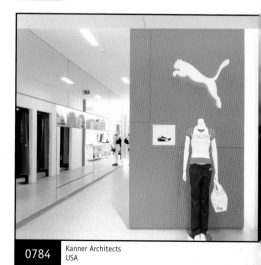

0784 Kanner Architects
USA

0785 Kanner Architects
USA

0787   JGA
        USA

0788   JGA
        USA

0789   JGA
        USA

0790   JGA
        USA

0791   JGA
USA

0792   JGA
USA

0793   JGA
USA

0794   Sayles Graphic Design
USA

0797 Life is good.
USA

0798 Miss Selfridge
UK

0799 Miss Selfridge
UK

0800 Miss Selfridge
UK

0801 Kracka
UK

0802 Kracka
UK

0803 Orne & Associates
USA

0804 Chute Gerdeman
USA

0805 Chute Gerdeman
USA

0806 Chute Gerdeman
USA

0807 Cherie Yeo Architects & Design
UK

0808 Cherie Yeo Architects & Design
UK

0809 Gardner Design
USA

0810 Gardner Design
USA

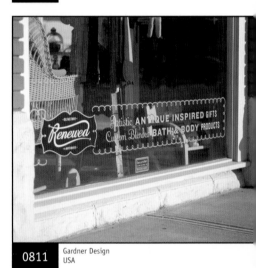

0811 Gardner Design
USA

0812 Gardner Design
USA

0813 Gardner Design
USA

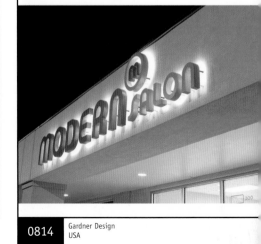

0814 Gardner Design
USA

Pyott Design Consultants
UK

JGA
USA

0817 JGA
USA

0818 JGA
USA

0819 JGA
USA

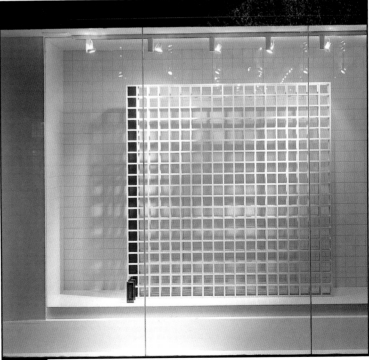

0820 Shiseido
USA

0821 JGA
USA

0822 JGA
USA

0823 JGA
USA

0824 JGA
USA

Curiosity
Japan

0827 Curiosity
Japan

0828 Gardner Design
USA

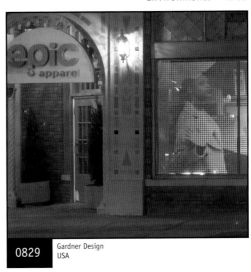

0829 Gardner Design
USA

0830 Gardner Design
USA

0831 Gardner Design
USA

0832 Gardner Design
USA

0833 Gardner Design
USA

0834 Gardner Design
USA

0835 JGA
USA

0836 Parham Santana
USA

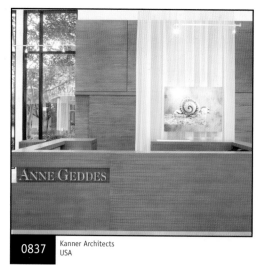

0837 Kanner Architects
USA

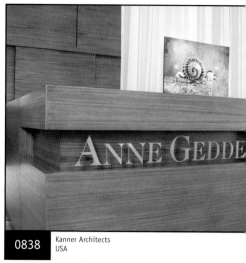

0838 Kanner Architects
USA

0839 AdamsMorioka
USA

0840 Fitch
USA

0841 Fitch
USA

0842 Morla Design
USA

0843 Gardner Design
USA

0844 Gardner Design
USA

0845   Kanner Architects
USA

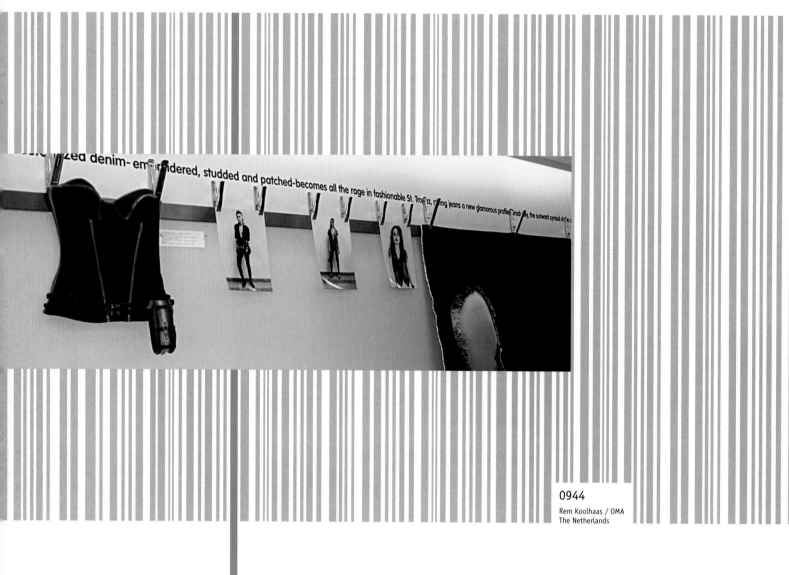

0944
Rem Koolhaas / OMA
The Netherlands

0 | 8 4 6

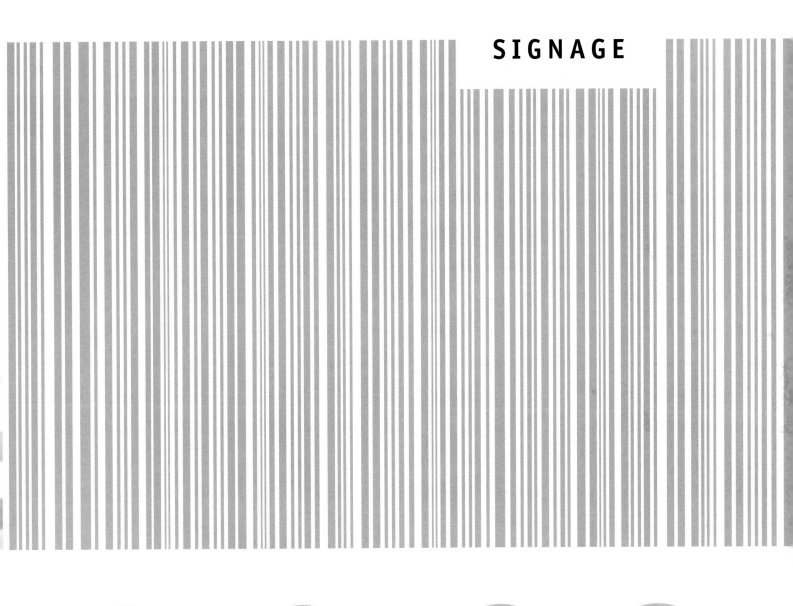

SIGNAGE

0 9 6 0

© Deering Photography

0846   Minelli Inc.
USA

0847 ° Minelli Inc.
USA

0848 Minelli Inc.
USA

0849 Minelli Inc.
USA

0850 Minelli Inc.
USA

0851   Ruben Esparza Design
USA

0852   Ruben Esparza Design
USA

0853   Ruben Esparza Design
USA

0854   Ruben Esparza Design
USA

Ruben Esparza Design
USA

TOP IT OFF

Ruben Esparza Design
USA

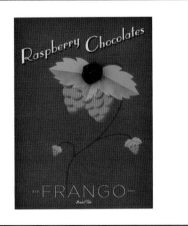

0857   Wink
USA

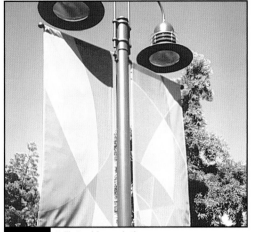

0858   Hollis Brand Communications
USA

0859   Hollis Brand Communications
USA

0860   Hollis Brand Communications
USA

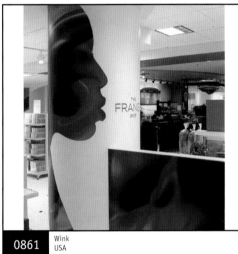

0861   Wink
USA

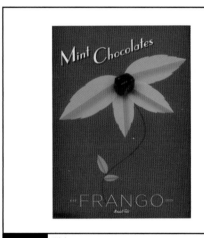

0862   Wink
USA

0863   Wink
USA

0864   Wink
USA

0865   Evenson Design Group
USA

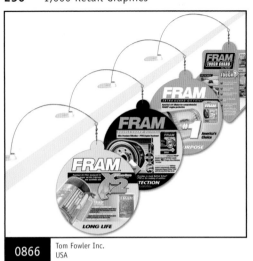

0866   Tom Fowler Inc.
USA

0867   Tom Fowler Inc.
USA

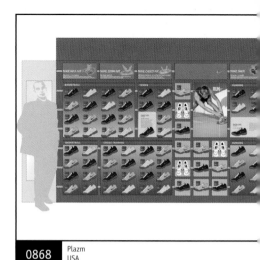

0868   Plazm
USA

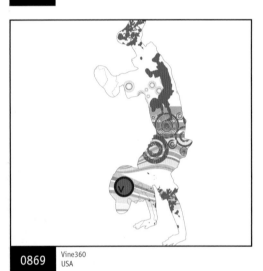

0869   Vine360
USA

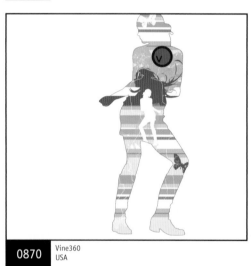

0870   Vine360
USA

0871   Vine360
USA

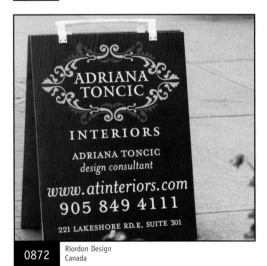

0872   Riordon Design
Canada

0873   Urban Influence Design Studio
USA

0874   Urban Influence Design Studio
USA

EAST END/
STRETCH
BOOTCUT

JAG

MID RISE
SLIM FIT

BOOTCUT
ZIP FLY

FIT

FEAT

MORFFEW
PHOTOSPH
MORFFEW
PHOTOSPH

0877 Landini Associates
Australia

Concierge
Herbal Treatments
Laundry
Sandwiches
Donuts
Bagels
Sushi

Delivery Area

0878 Landini Associates
Australia

0879 Landini Associates
Australia

stop and unwind
stop and unwind
bags of ideas

0880 Landini Associates
Australia

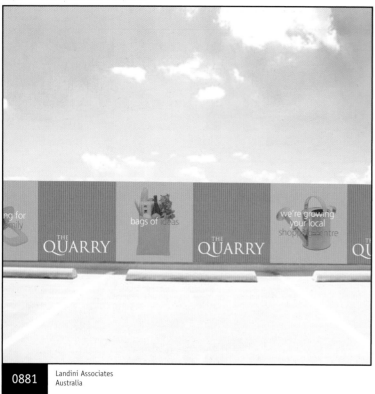

0881   Landini Associates
Australia

0882   Cubellis Marco Retail
USA

0883   Cubellis Marco Retail
USA

0884   Cubellis Marco Retail
USA

WL2 Studios NYC
USA

0887 S&N Design
USA

0888 WL2 Studios NYC
USA

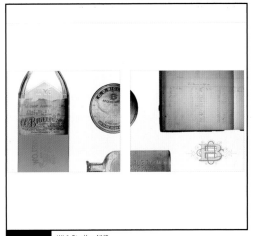

0889 WL2 Studios NYC
USA

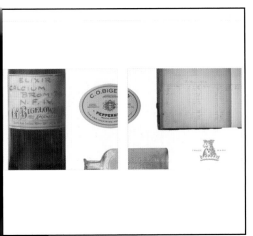

0890 WL2 Studios NYC
USA

0891 WL2 Studios NYC
USA

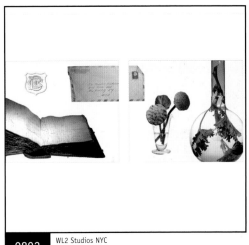

0892 WL2 Studios NYC
USA

0893 WL2 Studios NYC
USA

0894 Muggie Ramadani Design Studio
Denmark

0895 Muggie Ramadani Design Studio
Denmark

0896 Harcus Design
Australia

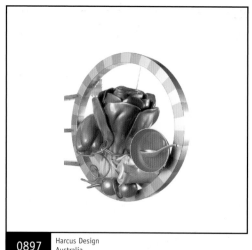

0897 Harcus Design
Australia

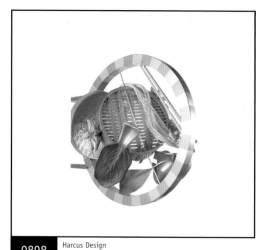

0898 Harcus Design
Australia

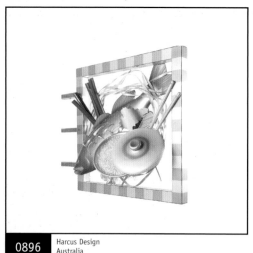

0899 Hollis Brand Communications
USA

0900 Hollis Brand Communications
USA

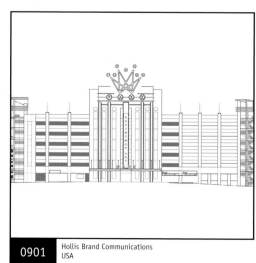

0901 Hollis Brand Communications
USA

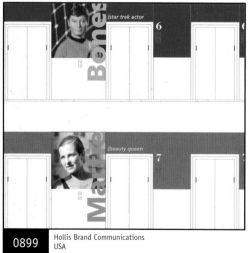
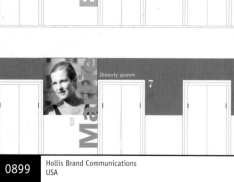

0902 Miriello Grafico
USA

0903 Miriello Grafico
USA

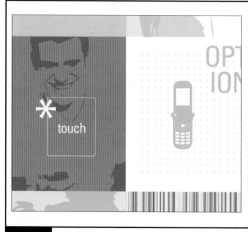

0904 Miriello Grafico
USA

Llénalo
por
menos

Cubellis Marco Retail
USA

0907 Cubellis Marco Retail
USA

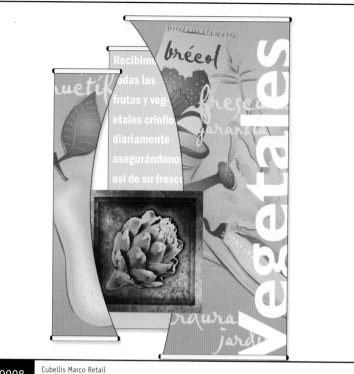

0908 Cubellis Marco Retail
USA

0909 Cubellis Marco Retail
USA

0910 Cubellis Marco Retail
USA

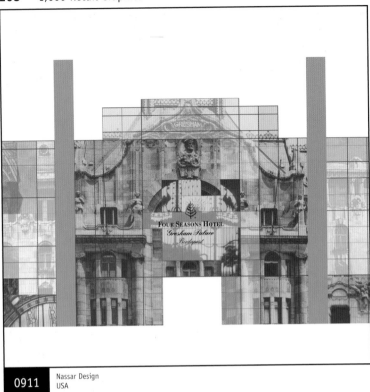

0911 Nassar Design
USA

0912 JGA
USA

0913 Hollis Brand Communications
USA

0914 Evenson Design Group
USA

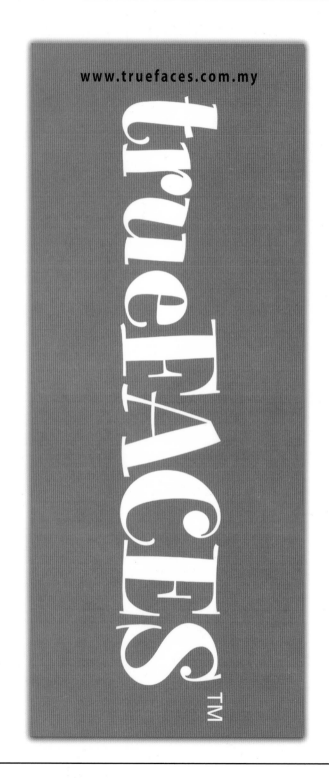

TrueFaces Creation Sdn Bhd
West Malaysia

| 0917 | R&MAG Graphic Design
Italy |

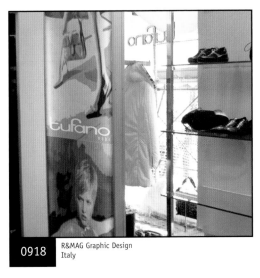

| 0918 | R&MAG Graphic Design
Italy |

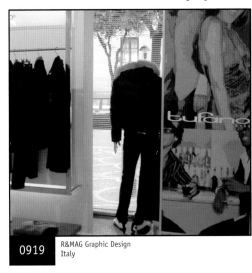

| 0919 | R&MAG Graphic Design
Italy |

| 0920 | R&MAG Graphic Design
Italy |

| 0921 | WSG Studio
USA |

| 0922 | WSG Studio
USA |

| 0923 | WSG Studio
USA |

| 0924 | Gardner Design
USA |

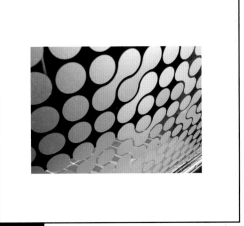

| 0925 | Gardner Design
USA |

0926
Diesel
USA

0927
Gardner Design
USA

0928
Gardner Design
USA

0929
Love Communications
USA

0930
Love Communications
USA

0931
Love Communications
USA

0932
Love Communications
USA

0933
Love Communications
USA

0934
Fitch
USA

Bad Studio
USA

Chute Gerdeman
USA

0937 Krispy Kreme Doughnuts, Inc.
USA

the warehouse sale

0938 Bad Studio
USA

SCHRŒDER
KNOW THE **DIFFERENCE**

speak your mind
drink your milk

milk

0939 Bamboo
USA

SCHRŒDER
KNOW THE **DIFFERENCE**

submit to
temptation

milk

0940 Bamboo
USA

0941 Rem Koolhaas / OMA
The Netherlands

0942 Rem Koolhaas / OMA
The Netherlands

0943 Rem Koolhaas / OMA
The Netherlands

0944 Rem Koolhaas / OMA
The Netherlands

TrueFaces Creation Sdn Bhd
West Malaysia

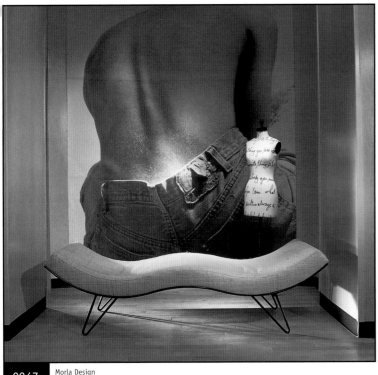

0947	Morla Design USA

0948	Morla Design USA

0949	Evenson Design Group USA

0950	Evenson Design Group USA

sky design
USA

0952 Wolken Communica
USA

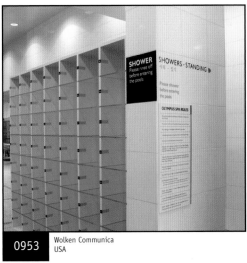

0953 Wolken Communica
USA

0954 Wolken Communica
USA

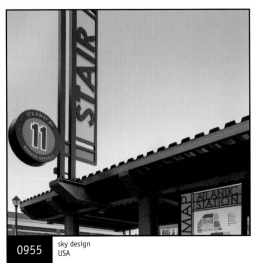

0955 sky design
USA

0956 sky design
USA

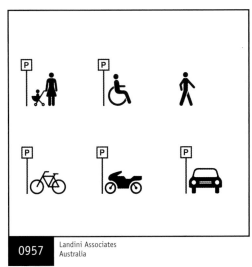

0957 Landini Associates
Australia

0958 Landini Associates
Australia

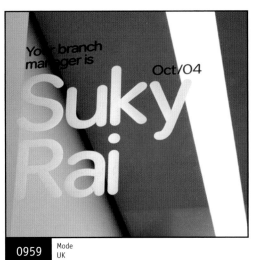

0959 Mode
UK

0960 Mode
UK

0969
Aloof Design
UK

0961

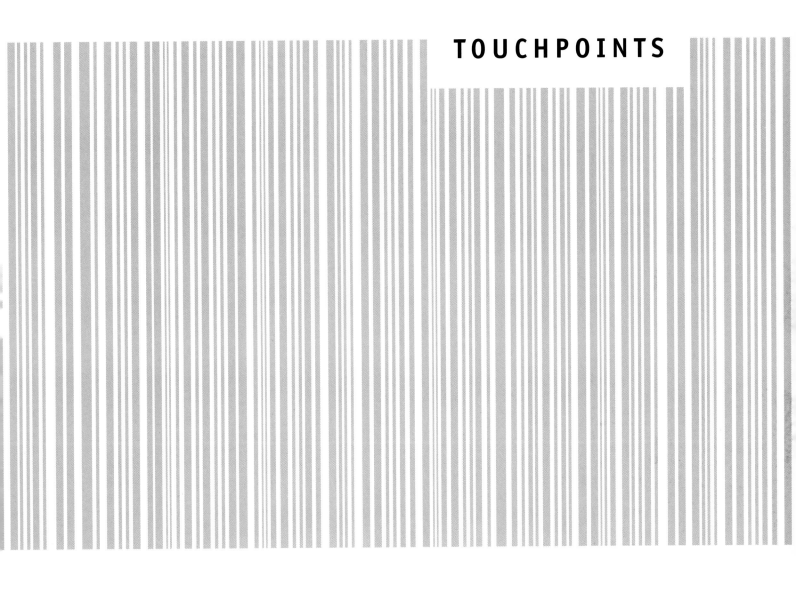

TOUCHPOINTS

1000

ready and
willing.

D'lush

fashion valley mall

7007 friars road suite 915 san diego CA 92108

619.987.5400

M THE PRESS

LUSCIOUS LEMONADE	2.75
STRAWBERRY SENSATION	3.50
VANILLA VANITY	3.00
BIG O!	3.25

FROM THE FOUNTAIN — 2.75

S1 CHERRY POP!	2.75
S2 OLD-FASHIONED ROOT BEER FLOAT	2.75
S3 ORANGE FRESHY	3.25
S4 MOCHA SATIN SODA	3.25

C2 CAPPUCCINO		
C3 LATTE		
C4 VANILLA MACHIATO	2.50	3.00
C5 HOT CRÈME CARAMEL	2.75	3.25
C6 HOTTIE CHOCOLATE	2.75	3.25
	2.75	3.00

T3 BABUSHKA'S FAVOR...		
T4 SPICED APPLE CIDER	2.50	2.75

D'lush

D4 PEANUT BUTTER ...	75
D5 CHOCOLATE HAZELNUT	2.75
D6 LITE VEGGIE	2.75
D7 CINNAMON TOAST	2.75
D8 RASPBERRY SWIRL	2.75

CHILL-OUT

C7 MOCHA FRAPPE	3.75
C8 D'LUSH FRAPPE	3.25
C9 COFFEE ON THE ROCKS	3.25
C10 CARAMEL ICE	2.00
C11 ICY COLD MILK	3.50
	1.50

ICY

T5 NAKED ANGEL ICED TEA	2.75
T6 I.B.'S THAI ICED TEA	3.25
T7 CHAI CHILL	2.75
T8 MANGO PEARL TEA	3.25
T9 GREEN PEARL TEA	3.25

YOUR WISH IS OUR D'MAND

D10 PICK YOUR PLEASURE	0.35

SHAKE IT

S5 BANANA BUBBLE	3.75
S6 BERRY BUBBLE	4.00
S7 COOKIES & CREAM	3.50
S8 ALOT-A-COLADA	

MOOTHIES

X'T'C	3.50
GRAPE ESCAPE	4.00
PEANUT POWER	3.75
T'LUSH	3.75
RASPBERRY RIP	3.75

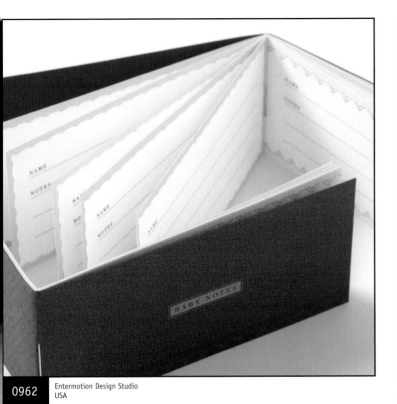

0962 Entermotion Design Studio
USA

0963 Landini Associates
Australia

0964 Landini Associates
Australia

0965 Nocturnal Graphic Design Studio
USA

0966   Epos, Inc.
USA

0967   Hollis Brand Communications
USA

0968   Greenmelon Inc.
Canada

0969   Aloof Design
UK

Taxi Studio Ltd.
UK

Evenson Design Group
USA

0972	Muggie Ramadani Design Studio Denmark

0973	Fauxkoi Design Co. USA

0974	Miriello Grafico USA

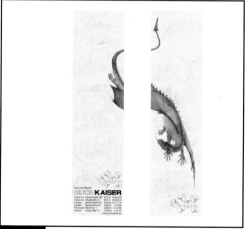

0975	Finest-Magma Brand Design Germany

0976	Ideas Frescas (Fresh Ideas) El Salvador

0977	New Pioneer Food Co-op USA

0978	New Pioneer Food Co-op USA

0979	Bamboo USA

0980	Desgrippes Gobé USA

| 0981 | Gardner Design
USA |

| 0982 | Gardner Design
USA |

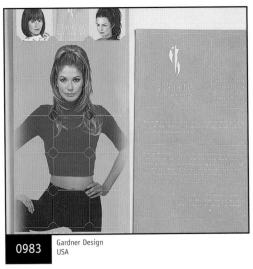

| 0983 | Gardner Design
USA |

| 0984 | Life is good.
USA |

| 0985 | Life is good.
USA |

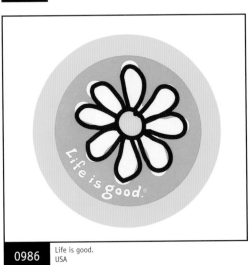

| 0986 | Life is good.
USA |

| 0987 | Life is good.
USA |

| 0988 | Hollis Brand Communications
USA |

| 0989 | Pentagram Design
UK |

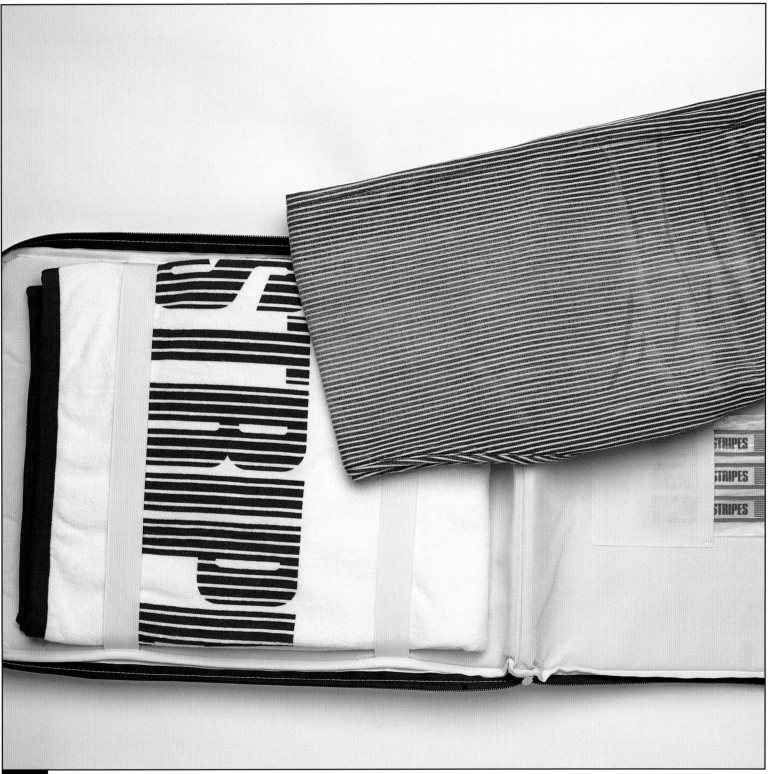

0990   Diesel
         USA

Diesel
USA

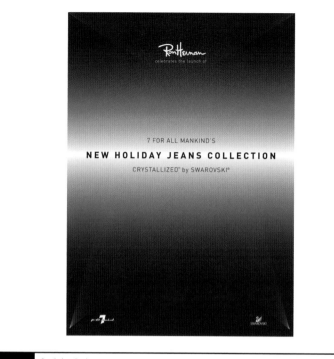

0992	Geyrhalter Design USA

0993	R by 45rpm USA

0994	Nita B. Creative USA

0995	Good Night TV USA

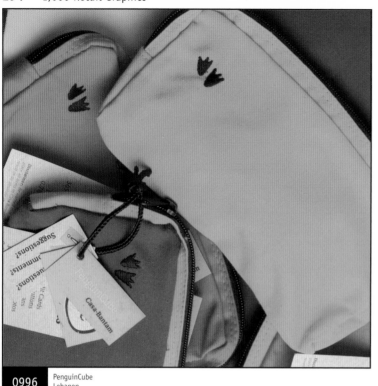

| 0996 | PenguinCube
Lebanon |

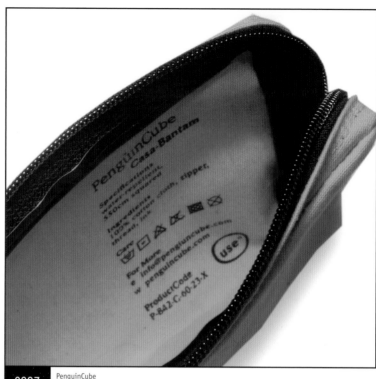

| 0997 | PenguinCube
Lebanon |

| 0998 | TrueFaces Creation Sdn Bhd
West Malaysia |

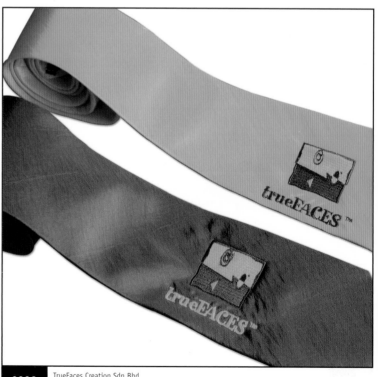

| 0999 | TrueFaces Creation Sdn Bhd
West Malaysia |

TrueFaces Creation Sdn Bhd
West Malaysia

DIRECTORY & INDEX

28 Limited Brand

Bessemerstr. 85,
Halle 8
44793 Bochum
Germany
+49 234 916095 1
www.twenty-eight.de

• 0106
   Art Director and
   Designer: Mirco Kurth
   Client: Vohwinkel

3

8220 La Mirada, Suite 500
Albuquerque, NM 87109
USA
505-293-2333
www.whois3.com

• 0006
   Creative Director: Sam Maclay
   Designer: Tim McGrath
   Client: Sack

3rd Edge Communications

162 Newark Ave.
Jersey City, NJ 07302
USA
210-395-9960
www.3rdedge.com

• 0102
   Art Director: Frankie Gonzalez
   Designer: Michelle Wang
   Client: Morlee's

88 Phases

8444 Wilshire Blvd., 5th Floor
Beverly Hills, CA 90211
USA
323-655-6944
www.88phases.com

• 0606
   Client: Soaptopia

9Volt Visuals

115 W. 4th St. #209
Long Beach, CA 90802
USA
562-688-1968
www.9voltvisuals.com

• 0312
   Art Director and Designer:
   Bobby June
   Client: 23 Skateboards

AdamsMorioka

8484 Wilshire Blvd., Suite 600
Beverly Hills, CA 30211
USA
323-966-5990
www.adamsmorioka.com

• 0515, 0839
   Designer: Sean Adams
   Client: Phillip B

A. Graphic Communications (AGC)

1350 Broadway, Suite 1209
New York, NY 10018
USA
212-967-9651
www.agcny.com

• 0373, 0374, 0375, 0376, 0377,
   0378
   Art Director: Pini Alon
   Designer: Ron Alon
   Client: 3v Company

Alison Goudreault, Inc.

Atlanta, GA 30303
USA

• 0294
   Art Director and Designer:
   Alison Goudreault
   Client: Bloomer's Upholstery

Aloof Design

Sam Aloof
5 Fisher St.
Lewes BN7 2DG
East Sussex
UK
+44 (0) 1273 470 887
www.aloofdesign.com

• 0274, 0389, 0671, 0678
   Art Director: Sam Aloof
   Designers: A. Scrase and
   J. Hodkinson
   Client: Elias & Grace

• 0327
   Art Director: Sam Aloof
   Designers:
   A. Scrase and J. Hodkinson
   Client: Georgina Goodman

• 0969
   Art Director: Sam Aloof
   Client: Georgina Goodman

ALR Design

2701 Edgewood Ave.
Richmond, VA 23222
USA
804-321-6677
www.alrdesign.com

• 0048
   Art Director: Noah Scalin
   Client: Metamorphosis

Anders Malmströmer Grafisk Design/AMGD

Anders Malmströmer
Skeppargatan 18
SE-114 52 Stockholm
Sweden
+46 (0) 70-722 64 01
a.malmstromer@telia.com

• 0140, 0649
   Art Director: Anders Malmströmer
   Designer: Anders Malmströmer
   Client: Svenskt Tenn

Animus Comunicação

Ladeira do Ascurra 115-A
Rio de Janeiro 22241-320, RJ
Brazil

- **0282, 0283**
  Art Director: Rique Nitzsche
  Designers: Rique Nitzsche
  and Felício Torres
  Client: Less Money

Apple Graphics & Advertising of Merrick, Inc.

8 Merrick Rd.
Merrick, NY 11566
USA
516-868-1919

- **0291**
  Designer: Allison Blair Schneider
  Client: The Aroma Boutique

Arcadia Studio

Isabelle Guerin-Groelz
2453 Lombard St., Suite 101
San Francisco, CA 94123
USA
415-794-1009
www.arcadiastudiosf.com

- **0035, 0548, 0549, 0552,**
  0553, 0554
  Art Director and Designer:
  Isabelle Guerin-Groelz
  Client: Red Ambrosia

ARTiculation Group

33 Bloor St., Suite 1302
Toronto, ON M4W 3T4
Canada
416-922-7999

- **0107**
  Art Director and Designer:
  Joseph Chan
  Client: The Shopping Channel

Bad Studio

1123 Zonolite Rd., Suite 18
Atlanta, GA 30306
USA
404-881-1977
www.badgraphics.com

- **0935, 0938**
  Client: Innovations

Bamboo

119 N. Fourth St., Suite 503
Minneapolis, MN 55401
USA
612-332-7100
www.bamboodesign.com

- **0092**
  Creative Director and
  Designer: Kathy Soranno
  Client: Best Buy

- **0939, 0940, 0979**
  Creative Director and Lead
  Designer: Kathy Soranno
  Designers: Jenney Stevens
  and Melanie Haroldson
  Client: Schroeder

Bartels & Company, Inc.

3284 Ivanhoe Ave.
St. Louis, MO 63139
USA

- **0290**
  Art Director: David Bartels
  Designer: John Postlewait
  Client: Cheapy Smokes

Baseman Design Associates

221 Mather Rd.
Jenkintown, PA 19046
USA
215-885-7157
www.basemandesign.com

- **0276**
  Designer: Frank Baseman
  Client: Aja & Alex

BC Design

Mike Calkins and
David Bates
116 S. Washington St. #2
Seattle, WA 98104
USA
206-652-2494
info@bcdesign.com

- **0615**
  Art Directors: Mike Calkins and
  David Bates
  Designer: Ryan Jacobs
  Client: Bugle Boy

Becker Design

Neil Becker
225 East St. Paul Ave., Suite 3000
Milwaukee, WI 53202
USA
414-224-4942
www.beckerdesign.com

- **0249, 0250**
  Art Director: Neil Becker
  Designers: Neil Becker and
  Mary Eich
  Client: tesserae

Brand Engine

80 Liberty Ship Way, Suite 1
Sausalito, CA 94965
USA
www.beplanet.com

- **0074**
  Art Director: Eric Read
  Designers: Eric Read and
  Coralie Russo
  Client: Cost Plus World Market

- **0075, 0076, 0077, 0078**
  Art Director: Eric Read
  Designers: Eric Read,
  Coralie Russo, and Lisa Brussell
  Client: Cost Plus World Market

- **0324**
  Art Director and Designer: Eric Read
  Client: inhaus industries

B.L.A. Design Company

521 S. Holly St.
Columbia, SC 29205
USA
803-518-4130
brandi@bladesignco.com

• **0408**
Art Director: Brandi Lariscy Avant
Client: Luna

Brandhouse WTS

10A Fredrick Close
London W2 2HD
UK
+44 20 7262 1707
www.brandhousewts.com

• **0181, 0516**
Creative Director: David Beard
Client: Tesco

Jake Burk

18959 Lina St. #908
Dallas, TX 75287
USA
580-763-3642
www.jakeburk.com

• **0009**
Art Director and
Designer: Jake Burk
Client: Tallulah Belle's

Casella Creative

1501 Front St., Suite 334
San Diego, CA 92101
USA
619-546-5286

• **0018**
Art Director: Chuck Casella
Client: Amy Hall
Designs

CFX Creative

259-3495 Cambie St.
Vancouver, BC V5Z 4R3
Canada
877-682-2914
www.cfxcreative.com

• **0108**
Art Director: Carly H. Franklin
Client: MedBizMarket

Charney Design

1120 White Water Cove
Santa Cruz, CA 95062
USA

• **0101**
Art Director and Designer: Carol
Inez Charney
Client: Village Bakehouse

Cherie Yeo
Architects & Design

24 Sunbury Workshops
Swanfield St.
London, E2 7LF
UK

• **0807, 0808**
Designer: Cherie Yeo
Client: Julie Verhoeven
Project: Gibo store interiors

chocolateTalk, LLC

34 R Spofford St.
Newburyport, MA 01950
USA

• **0631, 0646, 0647, 0682,
0683, 0684, 0685, 0686**
Designer: Silke Braun

Chute Gerdeman

455 S. Ludlow St.
Columbus, OH 43215
USA
614-469-1001
www.chutegerdeman.com

• **0598**
Client: LensCrafters

• **0599, 0612**
Designer: Steve Boreman
and Jennifer Lynn
Client: LensCrafters

• **0716, 0717, 0718, 0719**
Art Directors: Eric Daniel,
Elle Chute, and Eric Kuhn
Designer: Anne Fiorelli
Client: Sheetz

• **0731, 0732, 0733, 0734,
0735**
Art Director: Brian Shafley
Designers: Brian Shafley and
Steve Boreman
Client: Mars Retail

• **0804, 0805, 0806, 0936**
Designer information not available
Client: Keds

cincodemayo

5 de Mayo #1058 pte.
Monterrey, NL
Mexico 64000
www.cincodemayo.com.mx

• **0119**
Art Director and Designer: Mauricìo
Alanis
Client: Phone City

Clark Design

1 N. Main St.
Honeote Falls, NY 14472
USA
585-624-3895
glennc@rochester.r.r.com

• **0663**
Designer: Glenn Clark
Client: Two Cows

Coach

516 West 34th St.
New York, NY 10001
USA
www.coach.com

• **0527, 0528, 0530**
Executive Creative Director:
Reed Krakoff

Colette

213 rue Saint Honoré
75001 Paris
France
+33 (0) 1 55 35 33 90
www.colette.fr

• **0752, 0753**
Designer information not available
Client: Colette

Comme des Garçons, Ltd

601 West 26th St. 14th Floor
New York, NY 10001
USA
212-604-0013

• **0751**
Designer information not available
Client: Comme des Garçons

Communication Arts

1112 Pearl St.
Boulder, CO 80302
USA
303-447-8202
www.commartsdesign.com

• **0001**
Art Director: Dave Dute
Designer: Dave Dute
Client: Forest City Ratner
Project: Ridgehill Village identity

• **0002**
Art Director and Designer:
Mark Jasin
Client: Value Retail
Project: Maasmechelen Village
identity

• **0003**
Art Director and Designer:
Mark Jasin
Client: Value Retail
Project: Fidenza Village identity

• **0004**
Art Director and Designer:
Mark Jasin
Client: Value Retail
Project: Ingolstadt Village identity

• **0005**
Art Director: Mark Jasin
Designer: Mark Jasin
Client: Value Retail
Project: Wertheim Village identity

Creative Spark

116 Bury New Rd., Whitefield
Manchester, M45 6AD
UK
+44 161 766 1331
www.creativespark.co.uk

• **0355**
Art Directors: Neil Marra and
Carl Sadd
Designer: Andy Mallalieu
Client: Limited Fashion

Crocker, Inc.

17 Station St.
Brookline, MA 02446
USA
617-738-7884
www.crockerinc.com

• **0613**
Art Director: Bruce Crocker
Client: Planet Krunch

Cubellis Marco Retail

235 E. Main St., Suite 107
Northville, MI 48167
USA
248-374-2360
www.cubellis.com

• **0037**
Art Director: Julie Dugas
Designer: Mike Juras
Client: Amore Cooking Center

• **0038**
Art Director: Julie Dugas
Designer: Mike Juras
Client: Fiamma Grille

• **0882, 0883**
Art Director: Julie Dugas
Designer: Mike Juras
Client: Newton Farms

• **0884, 0907**
Art Director: Julie Dugas
Designer: Mike Juras
Client: Sentry Foods

• **0906, 0908, 0909, 0910**
Art Director: Andrew Bourdon
Designer: Mike Juras
Client: Bravo
Supermercado

Curiosity

Gwenael Nicolas
2-13-16 Tomigaya
Shibuya, Tokyo, 151-0063
Japan
+81-3-5452-0095
www.curiosity.jp

• **0826, 0827**
Art Director: Gwenael Nicolas
Designer: Kaoru Mizuno
Client: UNIQLO Co., Ltd.

D/Fab

32400 Industrial Dr.
Madison Heights, MI 48071
USA
248-597-0988
www.dfabdesign.com

• **0711**
Art Director: Debora Chin
Designer: Paul Hilpert
Client: Greyhound Lines, Inc.

delphine

P.O. Box 2802
Rancho Santa Fe, CA 92067
USA
858-759-7181
www.delphinepress.com

- 0241, 0358, 0359
Art Director and Designer: Erika
Firm
Illustrator: Eve Gray
Client: Trappings, Inc.

Design Bridge Ltd.

18 Clerkenwell Close
London ECIR 0QN
UK
+44 20 7814 9922
www.designbridge.co.uk

- 0513, 0514
Creative Director: Graham Shearsby
Client: Adnams Brewery

Design Center

15119 Minnetonka Blvd.
Minnetonka, MN 55345
USA
952-933-9766
dc@design-center.com

- 0247
Art Director: John Reger
Designer: Sherwin Schwartzrock
Client: Cameleon

- 0315, 0316
Art Director: John Reger
Designer: Sherwin Schwartzrock
Client: AvonLea

The Design Company

3130 East Shadowland Ave.
Atlanta, GA 30305
USA

- 0310, 0311
Art Director: Marcia Romanuck
Client: Epic Hair Design

Design Nut, LLC

3716 Lawrence Ave.
Kensington, MD 20895
USA
301-942-2360
www.designnut.com

- 0485, 0486, 0723
Art Director and Designer:
Brent M. Almond
Client: Timothy Paul
Carpets + Textiles

design hoch drei GmbH & Co. KG

Hallstrasse 25a
70376 Stuttgart
Germany
+49 711 5503 7730
www.design-hoch-drei.de

- 0651, 0652, 0653, 0654
Art Director: W. Shäffer and
S. Wacker
Designer: M. Wichmann, A. Stertzig,
and R. Pupillo
Client: design hoch drei
GmbH & Co. KG

Design Ranch

1600 Summit St.
Kansas City, MO 64108
USA
816-472-8668
www.design-ranch.com

- 0010, 0215, 0220, 0333,
0334, 0363, 0365, 0641
Art Directors: Michelle Sonderegger
and Ingrid Sidie
Designer: Tad Carpenter
Client: Bennett Schneider

- 0030, 0144, 0266, 0267,
0268, 0361, 0362, 0392
Art Directors: Michelle Sonderegger
and Ingrid Sidie
Designer: Tad Carpenter
Client: Fruit by Design

- 0121, 0122
Art Directors: Michelle Sonderegger
and Ingrid Sidie
Designers: Tad Carpenter and
Rachel Karaca
Client: Lee Jeans

- 0143
Art Directors: Michelle Sonderegger
and Ingrid Sidie
Designer: Tad Carpenter
Client: The Buckle

- 0145
Art Directors: Michelle Sonderegger
and Ingrid Sidie
Designer: Brynn Johnson
Client: Lee Jeans

- 0146
Art Directors: Michelle Sonderegger
and Ingrid Sidie
Designers: Brynn Johnson, Tad
Carpenter, and Rachel Karaca
Client: Lee Jeans

- 0150
Art Directors: Michelle Sonderegger
and Ingrid Sidie
Designer: Rachel Karaca
Client: Webster House

- 0190, 0191
Art Directors: Michelle Sonderegger
and Ingrid Sidie
Designers: Tad Carpenter and
Brynn Johnson
Client: Lee Jeans

- 0195
Art Directors: Michelle Sonderegger
and Ingrid Sidie
Designers: Michelle Sonderegger,
Ingrid Sidie, Tad Carpenter, and
Rachel Karaca
Client: Lee Jeans

Desgrippes Gobé

411 LaFayette St., 2nd Floor
New York, NY 10003
USA
212-979-8900
www.dga.com

- 0051, 0052, 0501, 0744,
0745, 0980
Art Director: Lela Houston
Designers: Brigitta Bungard and
Lizzy Lee
Client: Payless Shoe Source

Diesel

770 Lexington Ave., 9th Floor
New York, NY 10021
USA
212-755-9200
www.diesel.com

- 0507, 0508, 0509
Design Team: Diesel In-House with
KesselsKramer (Amsterdam)

- 0926, 0990, 0991
Design Team: Diesel In-House

Dotzero Design

208 SW Stark St. #307
Portland, OR 97204
USA
503-892-9262
www.dotzerodesign.com

- 0605
Creative Director: Mike Crossley
Designers: Karen Wippich and
Jon Wippich
Illustration: Jeff Foster
Client: Bridgeport Brewing Company

Duck Soup Graphics, Inc

257 Grand Meadow Crescent
Edmonton, AB TGL 1W9
Canada

- 0292
Art Director and Designer:
William Doucette
Client: French Meadow Bakery

- 0317
Art Director and Designer:
William Doucette
Client: Sunbaked Software

Duffy and Partners

50 South St., Suite 2800
Minneapolos, MN 55402
USA
612-758-2495
www.duffy.com

- 0440
Art Director: Alan Colvin
(Duffy New York)
Designer: David Mashburn
Client: Fractal, LLC

- 0608
Art Directors: Kobe Suvongse and
Alan Colvin (Duffy Minneapolis)
Designers: Joe Monnens, Paulina
Reyes, and Carol Richards
Client: Façonnable

Ellen Bruss Design

2500 Walnut St., No. 401
Denver, CO 80205
USA
303-830-8323
www.ebd.com

- 0185, 0495, 0500
Art Director: Ellen Bruss
Designer: Jorge Lamora
Client: Cherry Creek Shopping Center

- 0192
Art Director: Ellen Bruss
Designer: Jorge Lamora
Client: Belmar

- 0221
Art Director: Ellen Bruss
Designer: Gary Wiese
Client: Belmar

- 0581, 0588
Art Director: Ellen Bruss
Designer: Charles Carpenter
Client: Belmar

David Eller

400 N. Church St., Suite 400
Charlotte, NC 28202
USA
704-564-8900
deller615@yahoo.com

- 0043, 0399
Art Directors: David Eller and
Quincy Brown
Designer: David Eller
Client: Capri Rose Apparel

Entermotion Design Studio

105 S. Broadway
Wichita, KS 67202
USA
316-264-2277
www.entermotion.com

- 0012
Art Director: Lea Carmichael
Client: Small Town Treasures

- 0013, 0198, 0366, 0962
Art Director: Lea Carmichael
Client: Marshmallow Kisses

- 0142
Art Director: Lea Carmichael
Client: Palomino Market

- 0246
Art Director: Lea Carmichael
Client: In The Sauce Brands

- 0337, 0338, 0356, 0357
Art Director: Lea Carmichael
Client: Go Wild

- 0367, 0368, 0369, 0370
Art Directors: Brian Cartwright and
Joe Morrow
Designer: Lea Carmichael
Client: Marshmallow Kisses

- 0437
Art Director: Lea Carmichael
Client: Happy Cow

- 0441
Art Director: Lea Carmichael
Client: Kate Lane

- 0496, 0497
Art Director: Melissa Carr
Client: The Original Bundle

Epos, Inc.

Gabrielle Raumberger
1639 16th St.
Santa Monica, CA 90404
USA
310-581-2418
www.eposinc.com

- 0417
Art Director: Gabrielle Raumberger
Designers: Christina Landers and
Brandon Fall
Client: Flower Clip

- 0658
Art Director: Gabrielle Raumberger
Designer: Brandon Fall
Client: Los Angeles Public Library

- **0672, 0966**
  Art Director: Gabrielle Raumberger
  Designer: Eric Martinez
  Client: Los Angeles Public Library

- **0659**
  Art Directors: Gabrielle Raumberger
  and Eric Martinez
  Designer: Brandon Fall
  Client: Los Angeles Public Library

Evenson Design Group

4445 Overland Ave.
Culver City, CA 90230
USA
310-204-1995
www.evensondesign.com

- **0019, 0949**
  Art Director: Stan Evenson
  Designer: Katja Loesch
  Client: Synergy

- **0020, 0950**
  Art Director: Stan Evenson
  Designer: Mark Sojka
  Client: Angel City

- **0031, 0664, 0914**
  Art Director: Stan Evenson
  Designers: Stan Evenson and
  Jon Krause
  Client: Cubby's

- **0645**
  Art Director: Stan Evenson
  Designer: Matthias Fischer
  Client: Jurassic Park/Universal

- **0865**
  Art Director: Stan Evenson
  Designers: Stan Evenson and
  Amy Hershmen
  Client: Girl's Room

- **0971**
  Art Director: Stan Evenson
  Designers: Stan Evenson and
  Mark Sojka
  Client: Cubby's

Fauxkoi Design Co.

Dan West
1224 Quincy St., Suite 220
Minneapolis, MN 55413
USA
612-251-4277
www.fauxkoi.com

- **0973**
  Art Director and Designer: Dan West
  Client: Catlick Records

fFurious

32A Sago St
Singapore 059025
Singapore
+65 6225 0887
www.ffurious.com

- **0297**
  Art Director and
  Designer: Little Ong
  Client: fFurious

Finest-Magma Brand Design

Südenstrasse 52
76135 Karlsruhe
Germany
+49 721 831422 0
www.finestmagma.com

- **0236, 0352, 0353, 0354, 0427,**
  0428, 0429, 0430, 0431, 0432,
  0433, 0434, 0435, 0561, 0674,
  0675, 0676, 0677, 0975
  Art Directors: Lars Harmsen and
  Ulrich Weiss

Fitch

1266 Manning Pkwy.
Powell, OH 43065
USA
614-841-2044
www.fitch.com

- **0632, 0633, 0840, 0841,**
  0934
  Designer: Fitch
  Client: Hush Puppies Co.

- **0766, 0769**
  Art Director: Eric Kuhn
  Designer: Paul Teeples
  Client: Merrell

- **0770, 0771**
  Art Director: Eric Kuhn
  Designers: Farrick Reischmon and
  MJ Pichard
  Client: Trump Exchange

Fitch Worldwide (London)

10 Lindsey St.
Smithfield Market
London EC1A 9ZZ
UK
+44 20 7509 5000
www.fitchworldwide.com

- **0182**
  Design Director: Simon Mariati
  Client: Nissan Europe

Forum Studio Creativo

Carlos Ochoa
Barranca del Muerto 329
San José Insurgentes
Mexico, D.F. c.p. 03900
+52 55 5062 5100
www.forum.com.mx

- **0348, 0636**
  Art Director: Carlos Ochoa
  Designers: Antonio Mejia and
  Israel Calderón
  Client: Chilpas

Frost Design

Level 1, 15 Foster St.
Surry Hills, NSW 2010
Australia
+61 2 9280 4233
www.frostdesign.com.au

- **0098, 0736, 0905**
  Creative Director: Vince Frost
  Design Team: Vince Frost, Anthony
  Donovan, Bridget Atkinson
  Client: Arte & Frank

Gabriel Kalach - Visual Communication

1000 West Ave., No. 1004
Miami Beach, FL 33139
USA
305-532-2336
proartgraphics@mac.com

- **0116**
  Art Director and Designer:
  Gabriel Kalach
  Client: Inca International

- **0117, 0118, 0345, 0504, 0505, 0506**
  Art Director and Designer:
  Gabriel Kalach
  Client: Dulce de Leche

Gardner Design

3204 E. Douglas
Wichita, KS 67218
USA
316-691-8808
www.gardnerdesign.com

- **0111, 0642, 0833, 0843, 0844**
  Art Director: Bill Gardner
  Designer: Luke Bott
  Client: Kroger

- **0112, 0277, 0813, 0814**
  Art Director: Bill Gardner
  Designer: Brian Miller
  Client: Modern Salon

- **0147, 0301, 0539, 0983**
  Art Director: Bill Gardner
  Designer: Brian Miller
  Client: Bravadas

- **0148, 0177, 0186, 0187, 0188, 0189, 0536, 0537, 0538, 0622, 0692, 0693, 0694, 0695, 0981, 0982**
  Art Director: Bill Gardner
  Designer: Brian Miller
  Client: Aspen Traders

- **0211, 0212, 0529, 0643, 0644**
  Art Directors: Bill Gardner and
  Brian Miller
  Designer: Luke Bott
  Client: Standard

- **0213, 0634, 0834**
  Art Director: Bill Gardner
  Designer: Brian Miller
  Client: Fringe

- **0278, 0279, 0339, 0340, 0341, 0627, 0628, 0629, 0829, 0830, 0831, 0832, 0924, 0925, 0927, 0928**
  Art Directors: Bill Gardner and
  Brian Miller
  Designer: Luke Bott
  Client: Epic

- **0623**
  Art Director: Bill Gardner
  Designer: Brian Miller
  Client: Windowsill Foods

- **0624, 0625, 0626**
  Art Director: Bill Gardner
  Designer: Brian Miller
  Client: Cox

- **0809, 0810**
  Art Director: Bill Gardner
  Designer: Brian Miller
  Client: Vizworx

- **0811, 0812**
  Art Director: Bill Gardner
  Designer: Luke Bott
  Client: Renewed

- **0828**
  Art Director: Bill Gardner
  Designer: Brian Miller
  Client: Big Dog

Gateway

14303 Gateway Place
Poway, CA 92064
USA
585-848-3401
www.gateway.com

- **0616**
  Client: Gateway

- **0773**
  Client: Gateway

Gee + Chung Design

38 Bryant St., Suite 100
San Francisco, CA 94105
USA
415-543-1192
www.geechungdesign.com

- **0639**
  Art Director: Earl Gee
  Designers: Earl Gee and Fani Chung
  Client: Applied Materials

Geyrhalter Design

2525 Main St., Suite 205
Santa Monica, CA 90405
USA
310-392-7615
www.geyrhalter.com

- **0141**
  Art Director: Fabian Geyrhalter
  Designer: John Tsai
  Client: Moonberries

- **0992**
  Art Director and Designer:
  Fabian Geyrhalter
  Client: Ron Herman

Good Night TV

1400 W. Devon #322
Chicago, IL 60660
USA
312-238-8673
www.goodnighttv.com

- **0041, 0235, 0379, 0380, 0648, 0995**
  Art Director and Designer:
  Antonio Garcia
  Client: Good Night TV

Grafik Marketing Communications

1199 N. Fairfax St., Suite 700
Alexandria, VA 22314
USA
703-299-4500
www.grafik.com

- **0079, 0080, 0295, 0540, 0618, 0619**
  Design Team: Michelle Mar, Judy Kirpich, Gregg Glaviano, Lynn Umemoto, Kristin Goetz, Jonathan Amen, Ida Cheinman, and Eric Goetz
  Production Team: Heath Dwiggins, Regina Esposito, Ivan Hooker, and Fabio Silva
  Illustrator: Alysia Orrel
  Sign Painting: Julie Miles
  Photography: SOTA Photography
  Client: Market Salamander

Graphic Content

600 N. Bishop Ave., Suite 200
Dallas, TX 75208
USA
214-948-6969
www.graphiccontent.com

- **0216, 0217**
  Art Director and Designer:
  Art Garcia
  Client: Bodum Café and Home Store

Graphic Culture

322 1st Ave. N., Suite 500
Minneapolis, MN 55401
USA
612-339-8271
www.graphicculture.com

- **0418, 0419, 0420**
  Designer: Chad Olson
  Client: Petals

Greteman Group

1425 E. Douglas, #2
Wichita, KS 67211
USA
316-263-1004
www.gretemangroup.com

- **0062**
  Art Director: Sonia Greteman
  Designer: James Strange
  Client: Abode Home

- **0286**
  Designers: Sonia Greteman and Bill Gardner
  Client: Eric Fisher Salon

- **0320**
  Art Director and Designer:
  Sonia Greteman
  Client: Eric Fisher Salon

- **0323**
  Art Directors and Designers:
  Sonia Greteman and James Strange
  Client: Furniture Options

- **0471, 0475, 0476, 0477**
  Art Director: Sonia Greteman
  Designer: Garrett Fresh
  Client: Abode Home

- **0713, 0714**
  Art Director and Designer:
  Sonia Greteman
  Client: Abode Home

Gouthier Design

2604 NW 54 St.
Fort Lauderdale, FL 33309
USA
954-739-7430
www.gouthier.com

- **0123, 0124, 0196, 0197, 0205, 0330, 0331**
  Art Director:
  Jonathan Gouthier
  Designer: Kiley Del Valle
  Client: Erin London

Greenmelon Inc.

30 Elke Dr.
Ottawa, ON K2J 2C3
Canada
613-277-3911
www.greenmelon.ca

- **0045, 0046, 0329, 0550, 0556, 0557, 0630, 0637, 0712, 0885, 0968**
  Art Director and Designer:
  Robert B. Smith
  Client: Farm Boy

- **0057**
  Art Director and Designer:
  Robert B. Smith
  Client: Love & Romance

- **0095, 0470**
  Art Director and Designer:
  Robert B. Smith
  Client: CD Warehouse

Harcus Design

Annette Harcus
3/46 Foster St.
Surry Hills, NSW 2010
Australia
+61 2 9212 2755
www.harcus.com.au

- **0896, 0897, 0898**
  Art Director: Annette Harcus
  Designers: Annette Harcus and Marianne Walter
  Client: Taipei 101

Hardy Design

Rua Araguari, 1541/05
Belo Horizonte, MG 30190-111
Brazil
+55 31 3275 3095
www.hardydesign.com.br

- **0039, 0202, 0203**
  Art Director: Mariana Hardy
  Designers: Andrea Gomes, Carolina Marini, and Mariana Hardy
  Client: Café Fina Flor

- **0042, 0155, 0156, 0157, 0465**
  Art Director and Designer:
  Mariana Hardy
  Designer's Assistants:
  Cassia Perocco and Laura Barbi
  Client: Essenciale

- **0044, 0047, 0207, 0208, 0393, 0469, 0574, 0688, 0689, 0704**
  Art Director and Designer:
  Mariana Hardy
  Designer's Assistant:
  Clarissa Campolina
  Client: Bernardi

- 0100, 0165, 0394, 0397,
  0398, 0668, 0670
  Art Director: Mariana Hardy
  Designers: Andre Coelho and
  Mariana Hardy
  Client: Brigite

- 0158, 0159, 0160, 0466,
  0467
  Art Director and
  Designer: Mariana Hardy
  Designer's Assistants:
  Cassia Perocco, Gabriela Abdalla,
  and Laura Barbi
  Client: Essenciale

- 0162, 0163, 0164, 0468
  Art Director: Mariana Hardy
  Designers: Andrea Gomes and
  Mariana Hardy
  Designers' Assistants:
  Alexandre Perocco, Cassia Perocco,
  Gabriela Abdalla, and Laura Barbi
  Client: Essenciale

Hartford Design

954 W. Washington, 4th Floor
Chicago, IL 60607
USA
312-563-5600
www.hartfordesign.com

- 0243
  Art Director: Tim Hartford
  Designer: Ron Alikpala
  Client: Wishbone

Helena Seo Design

1000 Escalon Ave., Suite 1012
Sunnyvale, CA 94085
USA
408-830-0086
www.helenaseo.com

- 0582, 0583, 0584, 0585,
  0586, 0587
  Art Director and Designer:
  Helena Seo
  Client: Ineke, LCC.

Helmut Lang Parfums

80 Greene St., 2nd Floor
New York, NY 10012
USA
212-331-1014
www.helmutlang.com

- 0749
  Client: Helmut Lang Parfums

- 0750
  Electronic Sign
  Designer: Jenny Holzer
  Client: Helmut Lang Parfums

Herman Miller, Inc.

Marketing
Communications Dept.
855 E. Main Ave.
Zeeland, MI 49464
USA
616-654-3000
www.hermanmiller.com

- 0305
  Art Director: Stephen Frykholm
  Designer: Brian Edlefson
  Client: Herman Miller, Inc.

Hermès

Paris
France
www.hermes.com

- 0510, 0511, 0609, 0610, 0611
  Client: Hermès

HG Design

1509 Briggs St.
Wichita, KS 67203
USA
316-267-6164
www.hgdesign.com

- 0073
  Designer: Matt Pierce
  Client: Thunder Eagle Cycle Shop

Hollis Brand Communications

680 W. Beech St., Suite 1
San Diego, CA 92101
USA
619-234-2061
www.hollisbc.com

- 0015
  Designer: Don Hollis
  Client: Neuhaus

- 0016
  Designer: Don Hollis
  Client: AIGA

- 0017
  Designer: Don Hollis
  Client: Tower 23 Hotel

- 0056, 0899, 0900, 0901
  Designer: Don Hollis
  Client: Queensway Bay

- 0109
  Designer: Don Hollis
  Client: Black Bird

- 0168, 0169, 0721, 0722
  Designer: Don Hollis
  Client: Tower 23 Hotel

- 0218, 0701, 0702, 0858,
  0859, 0860, 0913
  Creative Director: Don Hollis
  Client information not provided

- 0219, 0662, 0710, 0961,
  0967, 0988
  Designer: Don Hollis
  Client: D·Lush

- 0481, 0482, 0483, 0484
  Designer: Don Hollis
  Client: Hang Ten

Hornall Anderson Design Works

710 2nd Ave., Suite 1300
Seattle, WA 98104
USA
206-826-2329
www.hadw.com

- 0541, 0542
  Art Directors: Kathy Saito and
  Jack Anderson
  Designers: Kathy Saito, Sonja Max,
  Henry Yui, and Yuri Shvets
  Client: Emily's

- 0543
  Art Director: Lisa Cerveny
  Designers: Mary Hermes, Holly
  Craven, Belinda Bowling, Tiffany
  Place, and Mary Chin Hutchinson
  Client: Benjamin Moore

• **0544, 0545**
Art Directors: Mary Hermes, Lisa
Cerveny, and Julie LaPine
Designers: Mary Hermes, Jana Nishi,
Belinda Bowling, Lauren DiRusso,
and Elmer de la Cruz
Client: O.C. Tanner / Thanks.com

• **0589, 0590, 0591, 0592, 0593**
Art Director: Lisa Cerveny
Designers: Lisa Cerveny, James Tee,
Tiffany Place, Mark Popich, Jana
Nishi, Leo Raymundo, Yuri Shvets,
and Belinda Bowling
Client: Tahitian Noni

Huss | Büro für creative Massnahmen

Stierstrasse 7
12159 Berlin
Germany
+49 30 2363 9550
www.buerohuss.de

• **0269, 0270, 0364**
Art Director and
Designer: Ralf Huss
Client: angelo's

I. Paris Design

246 Gates Ave.
Brooklyn, NY 11238
USA
718-783-2240
iparisdgn@gis.net

• **0028**
Art Director: Isaac Paris
Client: Europe on the Corner
Jewelry Shop

Ideas Frescas (Fresh Ideas)

Edificio Eben Ezer
Nivel 3
Blvd. Sur Santa Elena
Antiguo Cuscatlan
El Salvador
+503 2248 7420
www.ideas-frescas.com

• **0558**
Art Director: Frida Larios
Client: Sweets—El
Palacio de los Postres

• **0724**
Art Director: Gabriela Larios
Client: Mimate

• **0976**
Art Director and
Designer: Gabriela Larios
Client: HealthCo

IE Design + Communications

422 Pacific Coast Highway
Hermosa Beach, CA 90254
USA
310-376-9600
www.iedesign.net

• **0252**
Art Director: Marcie Carson
Designer: David Gilmour
Client: Sunset Sound

• **0360**
Art Director: Marcie Carson
Designers: Jane Lee and Kenny
Goldstein
Client: Theresa Kathryn

IKEA

Älmhult, Sweden
www.ikea.com

• **0091**
Client: Ikea

Insight Design Communication

322 South Mosley
Witchita, KS 67202
USA

• **0322**
Art Directors and Designers:
Sherrie Holdeman and
Tracy Holdeman
Client: Clotia

Iron Design

120 North Aurora St.
Suite 5A
Ithaca, NY 14850
USA
www.irondesign.com

• **0603**
Design information not available
Client: Sackets Harbor Brewing
Company

Jack Spade

New York, NY
USA

• **0746**
Client: Jack Spade

Jeff Fisher LogoMotives

P.O. Box 17155
Portland, OR 97217
USA
503-283-8673
www.jfisherlogomotives.com

• **0050**
Art Director and Designer:
Jeff Fisher
Client: W.C. Winks Hardware

Jeff Labbé Design

218 Princeton Ave.
Claremont CA, 91711
USA

• **0285**
Designer: Jeff Labbé
Client: Conn Quigley

JGA

29110 Inkster Rd., Suite 200
Southfield, MI 48034
USA
248-355-0890
www.jga.com

• **0071, 0772**
Art Director: Brian Eastman
Client: Zehnder's Marketplace

• **0096**
Art Director: Brian Eastman
Project Principal: Ken Nisch
Client: Blue Tulip

• **0097, 0349, 0350, 0351,
0490, 0564, 0565, 0570**
Art Director: Brian Eastman
Project Principal: Ken Nisch
Client: Torrid

- **0099, 0390, 0487, 0563**
Art Director: Brian Eastman
Project Principal: Ken Nisch
Client: Metropark

- **0488, 0566, 0567, 0568, 0738, 0739**
Art Director: Tami Jo Urban
Project Principal: Ken Nisch
Client: Kirkland's

- **0562, 0791, 0793**
Art Director: Tami Jo Urban
Project Principal: Ken Nisch
Client: Laura Secord

- **0756, 0759, 0760, 0835**
Art Director: Brian Eastman
Project Principal: Ken Nisch
Client: Hershey's Chicago

- **0757, 0758**
Art Director: Brian Eastman
Project Principal: Ken Nisch
Client: Harris

- **0761, 0762, 0763, 0764, 0915**
Art Director: Brian Eastman
Project Principal: Ken Nisch
Client: La-Z-Boy

- **0765, 0767, 0768**
Creative Director: Michael Curtis
Project Principal: Ken Nisch
Client: Brookstone

- **0786, 0787**
Art Director: Brian Eastman
Project Principal: Ken Nisch
Client: Mikasa

- **0788**
Creative Director: Gordon Eason
Project Principal: Ken Nisch
Client: Yankee Candle Co.

- **0789, 0790, 0912**
Art Director: Brian Eastman
Project Principal: Ken Nisch
Client: Rocky Mountain
Chocolate Factory

- **0792**
Art Director: Brian Eastman
Project Principal: Ken Nisch
Client: Spencer Gifts

- **0795**
Creative Director: Michael Curtis
Project Principal: Ken Nisch
Client: The North Face

- **0816**
Creative Director: Kathi McWilliams
Project Principal: Ken Nisch
Client: Ross-Simons

- **0817**
Creative Director: Kathi McWilliams
Project Principal: Ken Nisch
Client: Lindt

- **0818, 0819**
Creative Director: Kathi McWilliams
Project Principal: Ken Nisch
Client: Godiva Chocolatier

- **0821, 0822, 0823, 0824, 0825**
Project Principal: Ken Nisch
Client: Pulte Homes/ Del Webb

Jill Morrison Design

4132 Hidden Valley Ln.
San Jose, CA 95127
USA

- **0321**
Designer: Jill Morrison
Client: A Show of Hands

Kanner Architects

Stephen H. Kanner, FAIA
1558 10th St.
Santa Monica, CA 90401
USA
310-451-5400
info@kannerarch.com

- **0776, 0777, 0778, 0779, 0780, 0781, 0782, 0783, 0784, 0785**
Client: PUMA
(PUMA photos courtesy of
PUMA North America and
PUMA International)

Kate Spade

48 West 25th St.
New York, NY 10001
USA
212-739-6545
www.katespade.com

- **0600, 0611**
Client: Kate Spade In-House

Kendall Ross Brand Development & Design

1904 3rd Ave., Suite 1005
Seattle, WA 98101
USA
206-262-0540
www.kendallross.com

- **0436, 0438, 0439**
Art Director: David Kendall
Client: Surfer's Quest

- **0452, 0453, 0454, 0455, 0456**
Art Director: David Kendall
Client: Bellevue Square

- **0457, 0458, 0703, 0705**
Art Director: David Kendall
Client: Lincoln Square

Kiku Obata + Company

6161 Delmar Blvd.
St. Louis, MO 63112
USA
314-361-3110
www.kikuobata.com

- **0067, 0068**
Designer: Amy Knopf
Client: Stoltz

- **0069**
Designer: Paul Scherfling
Client: Stoltz

- **0498, 0499, 0502, 0503**
Art Director: Kiku Obata
Designer: Teresa Norton-Young
Client: Grand Ole Opry

Kinesis

295 E. Main, Studio 5
Ashland, OR 97520
USA
514-482-3600
www.kinesisinc.com

- **0066**
Art Director: Shawn Busse
Designer: Natasha Kramskaya
Client: Red Snail

- **0070, 0406, 0494**
Art Director: Shawn Busse
Designer: Sabrah Maple
Client: Fabric of Vision

- **0372**
Art Director: Shawn Busse
Designer: Michelle Cheney
Client: Sweetgrass Natural Fibers

Kinetic Singapore

2 Leng Kee Rd.
Thye Hong Centre
#04-03A Singapore 159086
Singapore
+65 6379 5320
www.kinetic.com.sg

- **0512**
Art Directors: Roy Poh, Pann Lim,
and Leng Soh
Designer: Leng Soh
Client: Pulling Strings

Kirby Stephens
Design, Inc.

Kirby Stephens
219 E. Mt. Vernon St.
Somerset, KY 42501
USA
606-679-5634
www.ksdweb.com

- **0308, 0309**
Art Director: Kirby Stephens
Designer: William V. Cox
Client: Tater Knob Pottery & Farm

Kraka

+44 (0) 20 7620 2247

- **0796, 0801, 0802**
Managing Director (Design):
Vic Kass
Client: MyTravel Group PLC
Project: MyTravel Retail Megastores

Krispy Kreme Doughnuts, Inc.

370 Knollwood St., Suite 500
Winston-Salem, NC 27103
USA
336-726-8997
www.krispykreme.com

- **0094, 0617, 0774, 0775, 0937**
Client: Krispy Kreme Doughnuts

Lain Livingston
Marketing Studio

3595 Canton Rd., Suite A9 #191
Marietta, GA 30066
USA
404-550-5508
www.lainlivingston.com

- **0060**
Art Director and Designer:
Lain Livingston
Client: Scrappy Apparel Co

Landini Associates

Mark Landini
42, Davies St., Surry Hills
Sydney, NSW 2010
Australia
+61 2 9360 3899
www.landiniassociates.com

- **0029, 0271, 0656, 0880,
0881, 0957, 0958, 0964**
Art Director: Mark Landini
Designer: Hannah Surtees
Client: Henderson Global Investors

- **0032, 0727, 0728, 0729,
0878**
Art Director: Mark Landini
Designer: Clayton Andrews
Client: Harrods

- **0103, 0126, 0127, 0272,
0547, 0657**
Art Director: Mark Landini
Designer: Hannah Surtees
Client: Tarocash

- **0104, 0239, 0240, 0244, 0660,
0706, 0877**
Art Director: Mark Landini
Designer: Clayton Andrews
Client: Morffew Photos

- **0125, 0383, 0730, 0879**
Art Director: Mark Landini
Designer: Clayton Andrews
Client: YD

- **0223, 0421, 0422, 0655,
0725, 0876, 0963**
Art Director: Mark Landini
Designer: Clayton Andrews
Client: Jag Jeans

Landor Associates

1001 Front St.
San Francisco, CA 94111
USA
415-365-1700
www.landor.com

- **0034**
Art Director: Rachel Wear
Designers: Graham Atkinson and
Andy Keene
Client: FedEx Service

Lauriedesign

12, ch. des Roulets
1228 Plan-les-Ouates,
Geneva
Switzerland
+41 22 743 1940
www.lauriedesign.com

- **0007**
Art Director and Designer:
Laurence Menoud
Client: Kozaïk

LAYFIELD

Level 3, 230
Clarence St.
Sydney NSW 2000
Australia
+61 2 9269 0789
www.stephenlayfield.com

- **0115, 0673**
Art Director and Designer:
Stephen Layfield
Client: Palm Beach Couture

- **0161, 0414, 0573**
Art Director and Designer:
Stephen Layfield
Client: Bloodorange

- **0680**
Art Director and Designer:
Stephen Layfield
Client: Ardino

- **0681**
Art Director and Designer:
Stephen Layfield
Client: Stephen Baker Foods

- **0687**
Art Director and Designer:
Stephen Layfield
Client: The Green Frog

• 0392, 0691
Art Director and Designer:
Stephen Layfield
Client: BRERA

Le Chateau
Marketing + Design Team

5695 Ferrier
Montreal, QC H4PINI
Canada
514-738-1000
www.lechateau.ca

• 0551
Designer: Le Chateau Marketing +
Design Team
Client: Le Chateau Inc.

Lemley Design

2727 Fairview Ave. E, Suite F
Seattle, WA 98102
USA
206-285-6900
www.lemleydesign.com

• 0521, 0522, 0523
Art Director: David Lemley
Designer: Kim Toda
Client: Tully's Coffee

• 0524, 0525, 0526
Art Director: David Lemley
Client: Tully's Coffee

• 0576, 0578, 0579, 0580
Art Director: David Lemley
Designer: Brian Pirot
Client: Tully's Coffee

• 0601
Art Director: David Lemley
Designers: Kim Toda and
Coventry Jankowski
Client: Graces Kitchen

LG Productions

3484 Bullitsville Rd.
Burlington, KY 41005
USA

• 0287
Designer: Laurie Gillespie
Client: CMO Custom Floral

Life is Good.

Boston, MA
USA
www.lifeisgood.com

• 0113, 0797, 0984, 0985, 0986,
0987
Client: Life is good.

liNa

197 Henry St.
San Francisco, CA 34114
USA
415-990-5462
www.linaedin.com

• 0260, 0261
Art Director and Designer: Lina Edin
Client: D. Romeo

Lloyds Graphic Design

Alexander Lloyd
17 Westhaven Place
Blenheim
New Zealand
+64 3 578 6955
lloydgraphics@xtra.co-nz

• 0036, 0265, 0381, 0385,
0572
Art Director and Designer:
Alexander Lloyd
Client: Optimum Health

• 0296, 0302
Art Director: Alexander Lloyd
Client: Fleurs

• 0403, 0462
Art Director and Designer:
Alexander Lloyd
Client: MOA Beer

• 0555
Art Director and Designer:
Alexander Lloyd
Client: Tackleman Ltd.

Loewy

Paul Burgess
147 Grosvenor Road
London SW1V 3JY
UK
+44 (0) 20 7798 2098
www.loewygroup.com

• 0259
Art Director: Paul Burgess
Client: Edge Shoes

Love Communications

Preston Wood
533 South 700 East
Salt Lake City, UT 84102
USA
801-519-8880
www.lovecomm.net

• 0332, 0517, 0518, 0519, 0604,
0929, 0930, 0931, 0932, 0933
Art Director: Preston Wood
Designers: Preston Wood and
Amy Veach
Client: Orchard Street Market

Marc Jacobs

USA
www.marcjacobs.com

• 0611
Courtesy of Givenchy USA
(Nicole Ehrbar)

Mars Advertising

25200 Telegraph Rd.
Southfield, MI 48034
USA
248-936-2642
www.marsusa.com

• 0472, 0473
Art Director and Designer:
Mars Advertising
Client: Harman Becker

Matcha Design

3513 S. Richmond Ave.
Tulsa, OK 74135
USA
918-749-2456
www.matchadesign.com

• 0065, 0577
Art Director and Designer: Chris Lo
Client: Seasoned Chef

Mayhem Media

1939 S. Quebec Way, Apt. 407
Denver, CO 80231
USA
303-847-9225
www.mayhemmedia.com

• 0263, 0264
Designer: Eric Hines
Client: Mark Garcia/Downtown
Radiator & Automotive

Michael Calleia Design

573 6th St., Suite 7
Brooklyn, NY 11215
USA
718-768-3232
www.calleia.com

• 0054, 0055
Art Director and Designer:
Michael Calleia
Client: Stinky Minky

Michael Kors

USA
www.michaelkors.com

• 0611
Courtesy of Givenchy USA
(Nicole Ehrbar)

Mindseye Creative

21 B Anand Darshan
13 Peddar Rd.
Mumbai 400026
India
+91 22 2351 0062
www.mecstudio.com

• 0033
Art Director: Uttara Shah
Client: Maruti Jewelers

Minelli Inc.

381 Congress St.
Boston, MA 02710
USA
617-426-5343
www.minelli.com

• 0008, 0846, 0847, 0848,
0849, 0850
Art Director:
Margarita Barrios Ponce
Designer: Stephen Rowe
Client: Museum of Science (Boston)

MiresBall

2345 Kettner Blvd.
San Diego, CA 92101
USA
619-234-6631
www.miresball.com

• 0307
Art Director and Designer:
José Serrano
Client: Chaos Lures

Miriello Grafico

419 West G St.
San Diego, CA 92101
USA
619-234-1124
www.miriellografico.com

• 0049, 0559, 0560, 0974
Art Director: Dennis Garcia
Designer: Sallie Reynolds-Allen
Client: Boney's Bayside Market

• 0902, 0903, 0904
Designer: Dennis Garcia
Client: Sprint

Miss Selfridge

70 Berners St.
London W1T 3NL
UK
+44 (0) 20 7291 2424

• 0798, 0799, 0800
Creative Manager: Matt Moss
Client: Miss Selfridge

Mode

Phil Costin and Ian Styles
26 Middle Row
London W10 5AT
UK
+44 (0) 208 964 2444
www.mode.uk.co

• 0737, 0959, 0960
Art Directors and Designers:
Phil Costin and Ian Styles
Client: Abbey

Morla Design

463 Bryant St.
San Francisco, CA 94107
USA
415-543-6548
www.morladesign.com

• 0174
Creative Director: Jennifer Morla
Designers: Jennifer Morla and
Hizam Haron
Photographer: Lionel Deluy
Copywriter: The Curious Company
Client: The Curious Company for
Levi Strauss & Co.

• 0620
Creative Director: Jennifer Morla
Designers: Jennifer Morla, Angela
Williams, and Yoram Wolberger
Client: Discovery Channel Store

• 0842, 0947
Creative Directors: Brian Collins and
Eric Roos
Designer and Illustrator:
Jennifer Morla
Photographers: Shelia Metzner and
Cesar Rubio
Copywriter: Suzanne Finnamore
Client: Foote, Cone, & Belding for
Levi Strauss & Co.

• 0948
Creative Director: Jennifer Morla
Designers: Jennifer Morla and
Angela Williams
Photographer: Jock McDonald
Illustrator: Jennifer Morla
Client: Levi Strauss & Co.

Mucca Design

315 Church St., 4th Floor
New York, NY 10013
USA
212-965-9821
www.muccadesign.com

• 0343
Art Director: Matteo Bologna
Designers: Andrea Brown and
Matteo Bologna
Client: Su-zen

Muggie Ramadani
Design Studio

Sortedam Dossering 55
DK-2100 Copenhagen OE
Denmark
+45 26 70 89 89
www.muggieramadani.com

• 0120, 0166, 0210, 0256, 0400,
0474, 0666, 0720, 0894, 0895,
0972
Art Director and Designer:
Muggie Ramadani
Client: Rebel Hairdesign

• 0299
Art Director and Designer:
Muggie Ramadani
Client: Porte à Gauche

• 0478, 0479, 0480
Art Director and Designer:
Muggie Ramadani
Client: Mille-K

Nassar Design

11 Park St.
Brookline, MA 02446
USA
617-264-2862
n.nassar@verizon.net

• 0404, 0405
Art Director and Designer:
Nelida Nassar
Client: SE for Interiors

• 0690
Art Director and Designer:
Nelida Nassar
Client: The Chinese Porcelain
Company

• 0911
Art Director: Nelida Nassar
Designers: Nelida Nassar and
Margarita Encomienda
Client: Four Seasons Hotel/Gresham
Palace

Jon Nedry

505 30th St., #211
Newport Beach, CA 92663
USA

• 0289
Art Director and Designer:
Jon Nedry
Client: Classic Cigar Company

New Pioneer Food Co-op

Marketing Dept.
Jenifer Angerer and Mat Greiner
22 S. Van Buren St.
Iowa City, IA 52240
USA
319-338-9441
www.newpi.com
mgreiner@newpi.com

• 0180, 0183, 0184, 0346, 0347,
0491, 0492, 0493, 0977, 0978
Art Directors: Jenifer Angerer and
Mat Greiner
Designer: Mat Greiner
Client: New Pioneer Food Co-op

Nita B. Creative

991 Selby Ave.
St. Paul, MN 55104
USA
651-644-2889
www.nitabcreative.com

• 0994
Art Director: Renita Breitenbucher
Designer: Jessica French
Client: Nita B. Creative

Nocturnal Graphic Design
Studio

5455 E. Ron Rico Rd.
Cave Creek, AZ 85331
USA
480-688-4207
www.nocturnaldesign.com

• 0040, 0193, 0194, 0200, 0201,
0224, 0225, 0226, 0227, 0228,
0229, 0230, 0231, 0232, 0233,
0234, 0273, 0382, 0463, 0464,
0640, 0965
Art Director and Designer:
Ken Peters
Client: Barbwire Western Couture

• 0061, 0461, 0661
Art Director and Designer:
Ken Peters
Client: Moody Blues

Nothing: Something: NY

Kevin Landwehr
242 Wythe Ave.
Studio 3
Brooklyn, NY 11211
USA
646-221-9972
www.nothingsomething.com

• 0128
Art Director: Kevin Landwehr
Client: Saved

• 0129, 0130, 0152, 0204,
0335, 0388
Art Director: Kevin Landwehr
Client: Made Her Think

- **0151, 0153, 0154**
  Art Director: Kevin Landwehr
  Designers: Kevin Landwehr,
  Devin Becker, and Scott Campbell
  Client: Bing Bang

- **0328, 0386, 0387**
  Art Director: Kevin Landwehr
  Client: A + G Merch

- **0426**
  Art Director: Kevin Landwehr
  Client: Saved Gallery of
  Art and Craft

Orne & Associates

3517 S, Centinela Ave.
Los Angeles, CA 90066
New York, NY 10011
USA
310-397-9995
oa@orneassociates.com

- **0803**
  Developer: The Rouse Company
  Columbia, MD
  Design Architect: (in collaboration
  with Orne + Associates, Inc.) MONK,
  LLC, Laurin B. ASkew, Jr., FAIA
  Baltimore, MD and Altoon + Porter
  Architects, Los Angeles, CA

Parham Santana

7 West 18th Street
New York, NY 10011
USA
212-645-7501
www.parhamsantana.com

- **0597, 0836**
  Designer: Parham Santana
  Client: Barbie

The Partners Design Consultants

Albion Courtyard, Greenhill Rents
Smithfield
London EC1M 6PQ
UK
+44 (0) 20 7608 0051
www.thepartners.co.uk

- **0667**
  Art Director: Greg Quinton
  Designer: Sue Farrington
  Client: Saks Fifth Avenue

PenguinCube

Tammam Yamout
P.O. Box 113-6117, Hamra 1103 2100
Beirut
Lebanon
+961 1 740088
www.penguincube.com

- **0396, 0996, 0997**
  Art Director and Designer:
  Tammam Yamout
  Client: PenguinCube

Pentagram Design

11 Needham Rd.
London W11 2RP
UK
+44 (0) 20 7229 3477
www.pentagram.co.uk

- **0989**
  Art Director: Fernando Gutiérrez
  Client: Hermès

Phoenix Creative

611 N. 10th St., Suite 700
St. Louis, MO 63101
USA
314-421-5646
www.phoenixcreative.com

- **0293**
  Art Director and Designer:
  Ed Mantels-Seeker
  Client: Art Classics Ltd.

Plazm

P.O. Box 2803
Portland, OR 97208
USA
503-528-8000
www.plazm.com

- **0445, 0446, 0875**
  Art Directors: Joshua Berger and
  Pete McCracken
  Designers: Joshua Berger,
  Lotus Child, and Pete McCracken
  Client: Nike U.S./ Footlocker

- **0447, 0448, 0449, 0450,
  0460, 0868**
  Art Directors: Joshua Berger and
  Pete McCracken
  Designer: Todd Houlette
  Client: Nike Asia Pacific

Prada

Via Maffei 2
20135 Milan
Italy
+39 2 546701
www.prada.com

- **0344, 0520**
  Designer information not available
  Client: Prada

- **0594**
  Designer: Karim Rashid
  Client: Prada

Pylon Design, Inc.

445 Adelaide St. West
Toronto ON M5V1T1
Canada
416-504-4331
www.pylondesign.ca

- **0214**
  Art Directors: Scott Christie and
  Kevin Hoch
  Designers: Scott Christie and
  Erin Boyce
  Client: Periwinkle Flowers

Pyott Design Consultants

Unit 3, 170 Katherine Mews
Whytleafe, Surrey
UK
+44 (0) 20 8668 5558
www.pyott.co.uk

- **0815**
  Designer: James Pyott
  Client: Ormonde Jayne

R&MAG Graphic Design

Via del Pescatore 3
80053 Castellammare di Stabia
Italy
+39 081 8705053
www.remag.it

- 0058, 0740, 0741
  Art Directors and Designers:
  Fontanella, Di Somma, Cesar
  Client: K-Out

- 0059, 0742
  Art Directors and Designers:
  Fontanella, Di Somma, Cesar
  Client: Maxin

- 0110, 0917
  Art Directors and Designers:
  Fontanella, Di Somma, Cesar
  Client: Outlet Space

- 0170
  Art Directors and Designers:
  Fontanella, Di Somma, Cesar
  Client: Segreti Di Venere

- 0262
  Art Directors and Designers:
  Fontanella, Di Somma, Cesar
  Client: B-White Multistore

- 0489
  Art Directors and Designers:
  Fontanella, Di Somma, Cesar
  Client: HPG

- 0575, 0743, 0918, 0919, 0920
  Art Directors and Designers:
  Fontanella, Di Somma, Cesar
  Client: Tufano Boutique

R by 45rpm

169 Mercer St.
New York, NY 10012
USA
917-237-0045
www.rby45rpm.com

- 0395, 0993
  Chief Designer: Yasumi Inoue
  Client: R by 45rpm

- 0747
  Chief Designer: Yasumi Inoue
  Interior Designer: Shiro Miura
  Client: R by 45rpm

Rem Koolhaas / OMA

Heer Bokelweg 149
3032 AD Rotterdam
The Netherlands
+31 10 243 8200

- 0748, 0941, 0942, 0943, 0944
  Project Coordinator: Marcus Scäfer
  Client: Prada

Revoluzion
Advertising + Design

Uhcanostrasse 4
78579 Neuhausen
Germany
+49 7967 1467
www.revoluzion.com

- 0172, 0173
  Art Director: Bernd Luz
  Client: Town of Tuttlingen
  (Germany)

Riordon Design

131 George St.
Oakville, ON L6J 3B9
Canada
905-339-0750
www.riordondesign.com

- 0026, 0199, 0222, 0402,
  0459, 0872
  Art Director and Designer:
  Alan Krpan
  Client: Adriana Toncic Interiors

Roger Gefvert Designs

4282 Highway 89 South
Livingston, MT 59047
USA

- 0288
  Art Director and Designer:
  Roger Gefvert
  Client: Golden Ratio Sports

Roycroft Design

7 Faneuil Hall Marketplace
Boston, MA 02109
USA
617-720-4506
www.roycroftdesign.com

- 0167
  Art Director and Designer:
  Jennifer Roycroft
  Client: Rachel's Makeup and
  Brow Studio

- 0326
  Art Director and Designer:
  Jennifer Roycroft
  Client: Suna at Home

Ruben Esparza Design
(RED Studios)

1308 N. Havenhurst Dr.
West Hollywood, CA 90046
USA
323-656-5449
www.redstudios.com

- 0336
  Art Director and Designer:
  Ruben Esparza
  Client: Best Buy

- 0851
  Art Directors: James Bellante and
  Julie Dove
  Designer: Ruben Esparza
  Client: Macy's

- 0852
  Art Director and Designer:
  Ruben Esparza
  Client: Macy's

- 0853
  Art Directors: Lynette Chun and
  Ruben Esparza
  Designer: Ruben Esparza
  Client: Macy's

- 0854
  Art Director and Designer:
  Ruben Esparza
  Client: Macy's

- 0855
  Art Directors: James Bellante and
  Ruben Esparza
  Designer: Ruben Esparza
  Client: Macy's

- 0856
  Art Director and Designer:
  Ruben Esparza
  Client: Macy's

S&N Design

212 North Eighth St.
Manhattan, KS 66502
USA
785-539-3931
www.sndesign.com

• **0887**
Art Director and Designer:
Steven Lee
Client: Four & Twenty Blackbirds

Sam Smidt Studio

666 High St.
Palo Alto, CA 94301
USA
650-327-0707
www.samsmidt.com

• **0442**
Art Director: Sam Smidt
Designer: Sam Smidt
Client: M10 Boutique

• **0443**
Art Director: Sam Smidt
Designer: Xenia Choubina
Client: M10 Boutique

Satellite Design

Amy Gustincic
539 Bryant St., No. 305
San Francisco, CA 94107
USA
415-371-1610
www.satellite-design.com

• **0531**
Art Director and Designer:
Amy Gustincic
Client: ZOIC

Sayles Graphic Design

3701 Beaver Ave.
Des Moines, IA 50310
USA
515-279-2922
www.saylesdesign.com

• **0023**
Art Director and Designer:
John Sayles
Client: B-Flat Music

• **0024**
Art Director and Designer:
John Sayles
Client: Catch Some Rayz

• **0081, 0082, 0083, 0084,
0085, 0086, 0087, 0088, 0089**
Art Director and Designer:
John Sayles
Client: Phil Goode Grocery

• **0090**
Art Director: John Sayles
Client: Pet Kingdom

• **0318, 0319**
Art Director and Designer:
John Sayles
Client: Martin Crowder Hair Salon

• **0451**
Art Director and Designer:
John Sayles
Client: Lil Puss

• **0546, 0665, 0794**
Art Director and Designer:
John Sayles
Client: Alphabet Soup

• **0650, 0669**
Art Director and Designer:
John Sayles
Client: Iowa State Fair

Shiseido

900 Third Ave. 9th Floor
New York, NY 10022
USA
212-805-2385
www.shiseido.com

• **0607**
Creative Director: Taisuke Kikuchi
Client: Shiseido

• **0820**
Creative Director: Taisuke Kikuchi
Client: Clyde's Chemist (for Shiseido)

Silvia Vallim Design

Av. Princesa Isabel, 323, sl. 1107
Rio de Janeiro, RJ 22011-010
Brazil
+55 21 2295-1976
www.silviavallimdesign.com.br

• **0391, 0726**
Art Directors and Designers:
Silvia Vallim and Gustavo Paschoal
Client: Barber Shop

Skaggs Design

1262 Mason St.
San Francisco, CA 94108
USA
415-395-9775
www.skaggsdesign.com

• **0384, 0679**
Art Director: Jonina Skaggs
Designer: Samantha Edwards
Client: Lush Life Nail Bar

sky design

50 Hurt Plaza, Suite 500
Atlanta, GA 30303
USA
404-688-4702
www.skydesigngraphics.com

• **0696, 0697, 0698, 0699, 0700**
Art Director: W. Todd Vaught
Designers: W. Todd Vaught, Carrie
Brown, and Robyn Canady
Client: Delta Community Credit
Union

• **0951, 0955, 0956**
Art Director: W. Todd Vaught
Designers: W. Todd Vaught and
Carrie Brown
Client: Atlantic Station, LLC

Splash Interactive Limited

Ivy Wong
1103-33 Bloor St. East
Toronto, ON M4W 3H1
Canada
416-928-0465
www.spashinteractive.com

- **0254, 0255, 0257, 0258, 0281**
  Art Director and Designer: Ivy Wong
  Client: Faces Bridal Boutique and
  Beauty Spa

Studio Boot

Luijbenstraat 40 5211
BT's Hertogenbosch
The Netherlands
+31 (0) 73 614 3593
www.studioboot.nl

- **0251**
  Art Director and Designer:
  Perta Janssen and
  Edwin Vollebergh
  Client: Sacha Shoes

Taxi Studio Ltd.

93 Princess Victoria St.
Clifton
England
+44 (0) 117 9735151
www.taxistudio.co.uk

- **0209**
  Art Director: Ryan Wills
  Designer: Spencer Buck
  Client: Hamleys

- **0970**
  Art Director: Ryan Wills
  Designer: Spencer Buck
  Client: Clarks

Td2, S.C.

Isben 43, 8th Floor
Mexico D.F. 11560
Mexico
+52 55 52816999
www.td2.com.mx

- **0063**
  Designer: R. Rodrigo Córdova
  Client: Plateria Rafael

Templin Brink Design

720 Tehama Street
San Francisco, CA 94103
USA
415-255-9295
www.tsb-sf.com

- **0149, 0342**
  Creative Director: Gaby Brink
  Designer: Brian Gunderson
  Client: Target

- **0175, 0176, 0300, 0532, 0533**
  Creative Directors: Joel Templin and
  Gaby Brink
  Designer: Gaby Brink
  Client: Target

- **0238**
  Client: American Eagle Outfiters

- **0407, 0415, 0614**
  Creative Director and Designer:
  Gaby Brink
  Client: Dockers

- **0534, 0535**
  Creative Directors: Joel Templin and
  Gaby Brink
  Designer: Brian Gunderson
  Client: Target

Tesser

650 Delancey St., Loft 404
San Francisco, CA 94107
USA
415-541-1999
www.tesser.com

- **0602**
  Creative Director: Tré Musco
  Client: Pearls Olives

thinkDESIGNco

5543 S. Lewis Ave.
Tulsa, OK 74105
USA
918-746-0746
www.thinkdesignco.com

- **0237**
  Art Director: Jason Maddox
  Designer: Deanna Priddy-Taylor
  Client: Under the Sun Garden Center

- **0707, 0708**
  Art Director: Jason Maddox
  Designer: Clifton Alexander
  Client: Under the Sun Garden Center

Thomas Pink, Ltd.

1 Palmerston Ct.
Palmerston Way
London SW8 4AJ
UK

- **0611**
  Designer information not available
  Client: Thomas Pink

Thomson Course Technology

Abby Scholz
1 Avery St., 20 C
Boston, MA 02111
USA
617-482-4009
abbyscholz@yahoo.com

- **0131, 0132, 0133, 0134, 0135, 0136, 0137, 0138, 0139**
  Art Director and Senior Designer:
  Abby Scholz
  Client: Thomson NETg Press

Tom Fowler Inc.

111 Westport Ave.
Norwalk, CT 06851
USA
203-845-0700
www.tomfowlerinc.com

- **0444, 0866**
  Art Director: Mary Ellen Butkus
  Designers: Mary Ellen Butkus and
  Brien O'Reilly
  Client: Honeywell Consumer Products
  Group

- 0867
Art Director: Mary Ellen Butkus
Designer: Brien O'Reilly
Client: Honeywell Consumer Products
Group

Total Creative, Inc.

8360 Melrose Ave. 3rd Floor
Los Angeles, CA 90096
USA

- 0248
Art Director: Rod Dyer
Designer: John Sabel
Client: Farrier's Nature

Trainor Design

49 Orient Ave.
Arlington, MA 02474
USA
781-643-2283
www.trainor-design.com

- 0242
Designer: Sarah Lotus Trainor
Client: Wild Women

Trickett & Webb Ltd.

The Factory
84 Marchmont St.
London WC1N 1AG
UK
+44 (0) 20 7352 6089
www.trickettandwebb.co.uk

- 0280
Client: Floris London

TrueFaces Creation Sdn Bhd

21, Jalan USJ 9/5P
Subang Business Centre
47620 UEP Subang Jaya
Selangor Darul Ehsan
West Malaysia
+6 03-8023 2121
www.truefaces.com.my

- 0105, 0325, 0569, 0946
Art Director: TrueFaces Creative Team
Client: Jesslyn K Cakes Jakarta

- 0114, 0171, 0275, 0571, 0754,
0755, 0916, 0945, 0998, 0999,
1000
Art Director: TrueFaces Creative Team
Client: TrueFaces Creation Sdn Bhd

Turnstyle

2219 NW Market St.
Seattle, WA 98107
USA
206-297-7350
www.turnstylestudio.com

- 0014, 0416, 0638, 0709
Art Director and Designer:
Ben Graham
Client: Venue

Unreal

Brian Eagle
12 Dyott St.
London WC1A 1DE
UK
+44 (0) 20 7379 8752
brian@unreal.co.uk

- 0298
Art Director and Designer:
Brian Eagle
Client: Association of Charity Shops

Up Design Bureau

209 East William, Suite 1100
Witchita, KS 67202
USA
316-267-1546
www.updesignbureau.com

- 0072
Designer: Chris Parks
Client: Alan Mairs

Urban Influence
Design Studio

Henry Yiu
423 Second Ave, Ext. South
Suite 32
Seattle, WA, 98104
USA
206-219-5599
www.urbaninfluence.com

- 0027, 0873, 0874
Art Director and Designer: Henry Yiu
Client: Ticklefish

John Varvatos

26 West 17th St.
New York, NY 10011
USA
212-812-8000

- 0178
Design information not available
Client: John Varvatos

- 0179
Design information not available
Client: John Varvatos

VINE360

9851 Harrison Rd., #320
Bloomington, MN 55437
USA
952-893-0504
www.vine360.com
info@vine360.com

- 0025, 0206, 0869, 0870, 0871
Designer: Joy MacDonald
Client: Vision Dancewear

Visible Ink

678 13th St., Suite 202
Oakland, CA 94612
USA
510-836-4845

- 0284
Designer: Sharon Howard Constant
Client: Albuquerque Connection

Visionare

11 Mercer St
New York, NY 10013
USA
212-274-8959

- **0595, 0596**
  Designer: Stephen Gan
  Illustrator: François Berthoud
  Client: Visionare

Vivitiv

119 S. Main St., Suite 210
Seattle, WA 98104
USA
206-623-9294
www.vivitiv.com

- **0635**
  Art Director: Mark Kaufman
  Designer: Jacqueline McCarthy
  Client: Sue Huston Seattle

Voice Design

1385 Alewa Dr.
Honolulu, HI 96817
USA
voice@lava.net

- **0253**
  Art Director and Designer:
  Clifford Cheng
  Client: Keri Hauser

Vrontikis Design Office

2707 Westwood Blvd.
Los Angeles, CA 90064
USA
310-446-5446
www.35k.com

- **0021**
  Art Director: Petrula Vrontikis
  Designers: Eden Parrish and
  Petrula Vrontikis
  Client: ib4e Partners

- **0022**
  Art Director: Petrula Vrontikis
  Designer: Eden Parrish
  Client: Overbreak

Wallace Church, Inc.

330 East 48th St.
New York, NY 10017
USA
212-755-2903
www.wallacechurch.com

- **0053, 0423, 0424, 0425**
  Art Director: Stan Church
  Designers: Lawrence Haggerty (logo)
  and John Bruno (hang tags)
  Client: Russell Athletic, Inc.

Wave 3

Rhonda Harshfield
725 So. Floyd St.
Louisville, KY 40203
USA
502-561-4189
www.wave3tv.com

- **0093**
  Designer: Rhonda Harshfield
  Client: YES

Whitney Edwards LLC

P.O. Box 3000
Easton, MD 21601
USA
401-822-8335
www.wedesign.com

- **0064, 0303, 0304, 0401**
  Art Director and Designer:
  Charlene Whitney Edwards
  Client: Joshua Tree Gardens

Widmeyer Design

911 Western Avenue, #207
Seattle, WA 98104
USA
206-343-7170
www.widmeyerdesign.com

- **0306**
  Art Directors: Ken Midmeyer and
  Dale Hart
  Designer: Dale Hart
  Client: Rolling Cones

- **0313, 0314**
  Art Directors: Kevin Widmeyer and
  Dale Hart
  Designer: Dale Hart
  Client: Deer Harbor Marina

Wink

126 N. 3rd St., #100
Minneapolis, MN 55401
USA
612-455-2642
www.wink-mpls.com

- **0621**
  Creative Directors: Scott Thares,
  Richard Boynton (Wink), and
  Connie Soteropulos (Marshall
  Field's)
  Designer and Illustrator: Scott Thares
  Client: Marshall Field's

- **0857, 0861, 0862, 0863, 0864**
  Creative Directors: Scott Thares,
  Richard Boynton (Wink), and Neil
  Pstashkin (Marshall Field's)
  Designer and Illustrator: Scott Thares
  Client: Marshall Field's

WL2 Studios NYC

213 Park Ave. South
New York, NY 10003
USA
212-366-0607
www.wl2.com

- **0409, 0410, 0411, 0412, 0413, 0886**
  Art Director: Bill Hovard
  Designer: Lee Iley
  Client: Express

- **0715, 0888, 0889, 0890, 0891, 0892, 0893**
  Art Director: Bill Hovard
  Designers: Lee Iley and
  Zach Ferguson
  Client: C.O. Bigelow

Wolken Communica

Kurt Wolken
2562 Dexter Ave. North
Seattle, WA 98109
USA
206-545-1696
www.wolkencommunica.com

- **0011, 0245, 0952, 0953, 0954**
  Art Director: Kurt Wolken
  Designers: Julie Schneider and
  Ryan Burlinson
  Client: Olympus Spa

WSG Studio

(Waranaco Swimwear Group)
Ali Filsoof
6040 Bandini Blvd.
Los Angeles, CA 90040
USA
323-837-6537
www.warnaco.com

- **0921, 0922, 0923**
  Art Director: Ali Filsoof
  Designer: Tina Virani
  Client: Speedo North America

Wunderburg Design

Innere Laufer Gasse 11
90403 Nuremberg
Germany
+49 911 2355 5420
www.wunderburg-design.de

- **0371**
  Art Director and Designer:
  Thomas Fabian
  Client: Silhouetta

ABOUT THE AUTHOR

JGA has evolved to become one of the leading retail design, brand strategy, and architecture firms in the United States. Since 1971, JGA has built its reputation by helping retailers realize their visual marketing potential and attain leadership within their niche. JGA believes that bringing a creative idea into fruition and achieving success requires the integration of strategic clarity, competitive and market awareness, conceptual innovation, and a strong business sense.

As chairman, Ken Nisch works on an international scope with responsibilities that include client liaison and total project design for retail operators, manufacturers, and brand marketers. His knowledge and entrepreneurial insight into consumer markets are integrated into market and design strategy, conceptual positioning, visual communication design and logo/brand identity, and architectural development and implementation.

Recognized by numerous design competitions and leading international publications, JGA client projects include American Museum of Natural History, Brookstone, Godiva Chocolatier, Hershey's, Hot Topic/Torrid, Jaguar, Lenox Inc, The North Face, and Saks Department Store Group.

To learn more, please visit www.JGA.com.

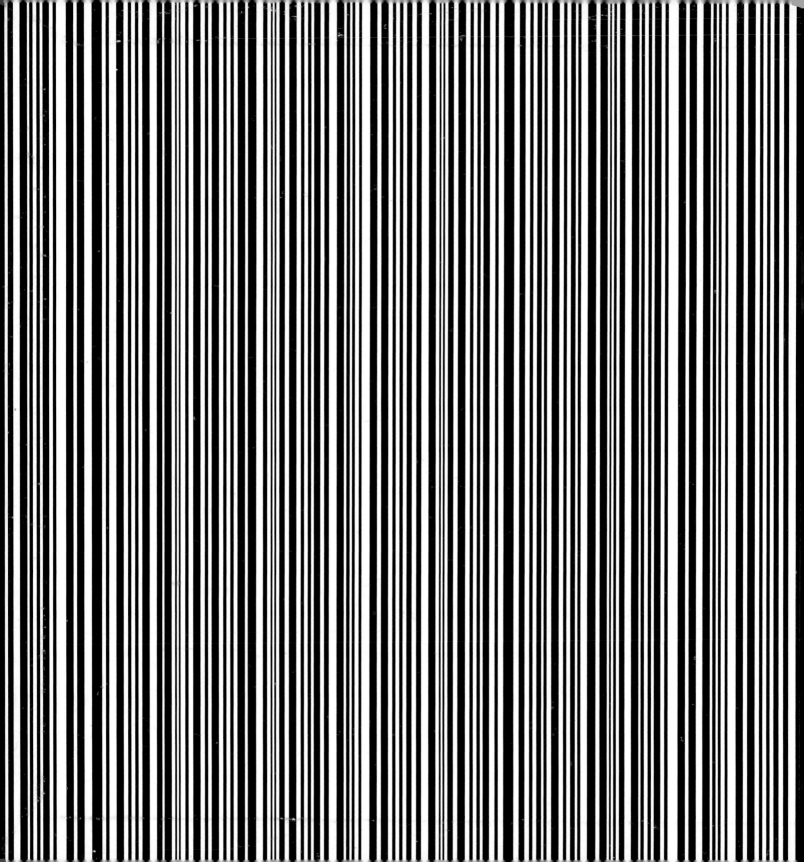